The MACAT Library
世界思想宝库钥匙丛书

解析G. E. M. 安斯康姆

《现代道德哲学》

AN ANALYSIS OF

G. E. M. ANSCOMBE'S

MODERN MORAL PHILOSOPHY

Jonny Blamey　Jon Thompson ◎ 著

陈广兴 ◎ 译

上海外语教育出版社
外教社 SHANGHAI FOREIGN LANGUAGE EDUCATION PRESS

目　录

CONTENTS

引言

要 点

- G. E. M. 安斯康姆是英国哲学家，因其伦理学 * 著作而闻名。
- 安斯康姆的文章《现代道德哲学》探讨日益世俗化的社会中的诸多概念，例如道德责任 *。
- 该文促进了道德哲学的现代化，对当代哲学中的伦理学进行了重新评估。

G. E. M. 安斯康姆其人

伊丽莎白·（G. E. M.）安斯康姆于 1958 年发表文章《现代道德哲学》，她是 20 世纪最重要、最有成就的哲学家之一。她关于伦理学和道德哲学的著作影响巨大，是当代行为理论 * 的开拓者。

安斯康姆就学于牛津大学，1941 年获得古典学和哲学学位；之后她在剑桥大学工作，在那里，她与奥地利哲学家路德维希·维特根斯坦 * 成为了朋友。她是维特根斯坦最忠实的学生之一，并在之后翻译了他的作品。维特根斯坦对她的影响很大：甚至在她回到牛津大学之后，她每周都会前往剑桥大学听他的课程。和维特根斯坦一样，安斯康姆以其敏锐的分析洞察力而闻名。

安斯康姆因其坚定的罗马天主教 * 信仰、性伦理学方面的保守观点，以及对核武器长期的反对立场而为人熟知。她反对避孕和同性恋行为，从而引发争议。她的思想促成了一个提倡贞洁和传统性价值观的学生组织——安斯康姆协会——的诞生，此协会在普林斯顿大学、麻省理工学院和其他几所大学建立了分会。她坚决反对第二次世界大战末期对核武器的使用，1956 年，她公开批评牛津大学对美国总统哈里·S. 杜鲁门 * 授予荣誉学位的决定，所列举的理由是杜鲁门批准在日本的广岛和长崎＊投放原子弹。安斯康姆认为，虽然投放原子弹能让战争立刻停止，从而减少了死亡总人数，但此举依然无可辩解，因为其目的在于杀害无辜平民。

《现代道德哲学》的主要内容

安斯康姆最重要的作品是她的文章《现代道德哲学》。她在文中开门见山地指出，此文包含"三个论点"：[1] 道德责任的诸多概念在世俗社会中已经毫无意义；英国主要道德哲学家（即后果论者＊，他们通过行为后果来判断行为的道德价值）之间并无本质差别；由于缺乏"充分的心理哲学"[2]，道德哲学成为徒劳无功的研究领域。

在其第一个论点上，安斯康姆认为有些概念是基督教传统的残余物，只有基督教传统才能制定道德规范。这些概念包括道德责任、道德义务，以及将行为区分为道德上正确和错误的做法。作为虔诚的上帝信徒，安斯康姆并未否定上帝的权威，而是认为一个世俗的社会已经无法使用伦理学的语言。譬如，人们已经无法继续使用"应该"一词，或其他相关概念，如道德责任（我们基于道德标准必须完成的事情），因为就其本质而言，世俗社会已经与上帝相脱离。

"应该"表示一种道德权威发出的指令，在过去，这一道德权威就是上帝。而在世俗社会里，上帝已不再是能够规定我们以特定方式行事的唯一权威声音。安斯康姆认为，没有了这种与上帝的联系，此类词语和概念业已丧失其意义。

安斯康姆的第二个论点是，我们无法区分此前75年间的英国道德哲学家。她认为，在道德哲学中并不存在真正的分歧，他们所有的人都一致拒绝信仰上帝，而从根本上赞同后果论——即一切行为只有依据其预见后果，才具有道德意义，任何行为规则在特定条件下都可被打破。她认为，尽管当代道德哲学家宣称彼此不同，但他们都指向同一立场——即他们都有可能赞同处死一个无辜的人。

如果有持枪者告诉你，她将杀死 20 个无辜的人，除非你杀死一个无辜的人（而且你有充足的理由相信她），根据后果论者的观点，你杀死这个无辜的人是正确的，而你不杀死这个无辜的人则是错误的，因为杀死这个无辜的人的后果比不杀死这个无辜的人的后果更加可取。[3] 这与统治欧洲长达千年的基督教道德观完全相悖，根据基督教道德观，特定行为属于不道德行为，无论其后果如何。

最后，安斯康姆提出，道德哲学需要一种基于心理学的不同模式。她认为，排除了上帝之后，再也不存在关于道德对错的阐释，伦理学不再建立在神圣律法之上。她另辟蹊径，认为我们应该回到来自古希腊哲学家亚里士多德 * 作品中的世俗概念，例如实践推理、德性和正义。因此，一个行为将不再是道德上错误的行为，而将是不正义的行为。德性伦理学 *——一种伦理学立场，根据是否获得或遵循诸如正义、睿智和慷慨等德性来判断生活是否向善——可以在非道德意义上存在，而无需上帝的权威。

《现代道德哲学》的学术价值

安斯康姆在很多领域都做出了卓越的贡献，包括行为理论（一个哲学分支，研究人类行为的本质）、形而上学 *（研究现实的终极本质），以及维特根斯坦的著作。她的文章《现代道德哲学》尤其具有重要的意义，因为它对伦理学产生了持久的影响。这篇文章使得一门名为德性伦理学的道德哲学流派重焕生机，后来的很多哲学家探讨了她在此文中提出的概念和道德问题。其中最著名的研

究者和作品有：英国哲学家菲利帕·富特 * 及其《美德与罪恶》，[4]
极具影响力的苏格兰哲学家阿拉斯戴尔·麦金太尔 * 及其《追寻美德》，[5] 奥克兰大学著名的德性伦理学家罗莎琳德·赫斯特豪斯 * 及其《美德伦理学》。[6]

安斯康姆的文章还从根本上讨论了道德行为对哲学的重要性和伦理学对哲学的价值等问题。她认为，除非责任、正义、德性等重要概念被彻底厘清，否则研究道德哲学毫无意义。此文呼吁一种全新的、更加清晰的思考方式，并要求哲学家们正确解释自己的术语和概念。

安斯康姆的文章促进了道德哲学的革新。在此文中，她批判了后果论和源自德国著名哲学家伊曼努尔·康德 * 的伦理学，认为它们要么不道德，要么缺乏内在统一性。后果论者认为如果处死某个无辜者可以带来某种整体性的积极后果，则处死该无辜者具有合理性，安斯康姆对后果论者的这种立场进行了批判。她认为这种思想是腐败的，并且一种更加广泛、更加普遍的人类道德标准不能取决于摇摆不定的多数派。

在当今世界，以追求更大福祉的名义而引发的国际冲突导致越来越多的平民伤亡，人们对此已经见怪不怪了，安斯康姆的描述提供了一种截然不同的道德标准。这一道德标准强调行为本身的正义、睿智或克制，而不是其后果。

---

1. G.E.M. 安斯康姆："现代道德哲学"，《哲学》第 33 卷，1958 年第 124 期，第 1 页。

2. 安斯康姆："现代道德哲学"，第1页。

3. 此例引自伯纳德·威廉斯和J. J. C. 斯马特：《对功利主义的支持和反对》，剑桥：剑桥大学出版社，1973年，第97—116页。

4. 菲利帕·富特：《美德与罪恶和道德哲学的其他文章》，伯克利和洛杉矶：加利福尼亚大学出版社，1978年。

5. 参见阿拉斯戴尔·麦金太尔：《追寻美德》，第3版修订版，伦敦：达克沃斯出版社，2007年。

6. 参见罗莎琳德·赫斯特豪斯：《美德伦理学》，牛津：牛津大学出版社，2001年。

第一部分：学术渊源

1 作者生平与历史背景

要点 ⌇

- 《现代道德哲学》改变了道德哲学*。此文批判了后果论者认为行为的道德判断取决于其后果的立场，以及来自德国思想家伊曼努尔·康德的伦理哲学，因为康德的伦理学建立在业已消失的概念之上，即道德责任（对个体做某事或不做某事的要求）。取而代之的是另一种道德理论，即现在所知的德性伦理学，它强调按照诸如正义、审慎和节制（适度）等美德行事。

- 伊丽莎白·（G. E. M.）安斯康姆是一个虔诚的天主教徒，在牛津大学和剑桥大学工作，其研究恰逢分析哲学*风靡学界的时候，分析哲学是指一系列强调对语言和概念进行分析的哲学方法。她是颇具影响力的奥地利思想家路德维希·维特根斯坦的得意门生，曾校对、编辑、翻译过他的作品。

- 此文写于第二次世界大战*结束不久，盟军——英国和美国所领导的军队——犯下的非正义行为，尤其是美国在日本的两座城市投掷原子弹一举，促使安斯康姆对当时盛行的后果论道德观提出了批判。

为何要读这部著作？

G. E. M. 安斯康姆的文章《现代道德哲学》[1]于 1958 年在《哲学》杂志上发表。安斯康姆在文中挑战了当时被奉行的道德哲学（对伦理学的研究）的基础本身。她提出，在对责任、正义、德性等重要概念进行透彻分析和理解之前，道德哲学毫无意义，并指责当代道德哲学家在使用这些没有任何明确意义的概念。她特别关注"道德责任"或"道德应该"的概念，认为这些概念来自基于上帝律令的伦理学观念——但这些概念很久以前就已经被哲学家视为基督教的历史产物而弃之不用。

换言之，当基督教在哲学领域逐渐被摒弃之后，道德责任概念日渐变得没有意义。哲学家在使用那些从本质上而言已经丧失其意义的词汇。

安斯康姆同时还发明了术语"后果论"来描述这样一种哲学观点，即对行为的道德判断只能通过考察其预期后果才能进行。她严肃反对这种观点和康德伦理学*，简而言之，康德伦理学认为，当且仅当你能让一个行为成为普世法则的时候，此行为才是道德的。所以，对康德来说，说谎话是错误的，是因为从理性上而言我们无法让任何地方的任何人在任何时候都说谎话。

最后，安斯康姆在文中提出的一些观点，最终形成了德性伦理学学科，此文的重要性可见一斑。

> "当前我们不可能从事道德哲学研究。"
>
> —— G. E. M. 安斯康姆："现代道德哲学"

作者生平

格特鲁德·伊丽莎白·玛格丽特·安斯康姆是一位校长和古典学者的女儿。她就学于西德纳姆学院，青少年时期读过大量的哲学和神学著作，结果成为一个虔诚的天主教徒。安斯康姆在牛津大学学习，1941 年获得牛津大学的古典学和哲学学位。本科学习结束之后，她同时在牛津大学和剑桥大学从事哲学研究工作。1970 年至 1986 年间，她担任剑桥大学哲学系主任。她最重要的哲学著作包括《现代道德哲学》（1958）、《意向》（1957）和《因果关系与决定》（1971）。[2]

安斯康姆于 1958 年发表《现代道德哲学》，当时她在牛津大学萨默维尔学院任研究人员。她曾是极具影响力的奥地利思想家路德维希·维特根斯坦的学生和挚友，1951 年维特根斯坦去世之后，安斯康姆成为他的作品的执行人。维特根斯坦对安斯康姆的影响体现在其主要的作品中，其中包括《现代道德哲学》。她与另一个天主教徒哲学家彼得·T. 吉奇*结婚，并与其育有 7 个小孩。安斯康姆的哲学著作以《现代道德哲学》最为重要，除了哲学著作，她还专门为天主教读者写过一些文章。

安斯康姆是一位著名的独立哲学家。1956 年，她公开反对牛津大学授予美国总统哈里·S. 杜鲁门荣誉学位，从而名声大振。她反对的理由是杜鲁门应该为二战期间在日本广岛和长崎投掷原子弹、大规模杀伤民众而负责。此前有人认为杜鲁门的行为合乎情理，因为虽然原子弹杀死了数十万日本平民，却有可能阻止了更多美国和日本士兵的伤亡。然而，安斯康姆并不认为这是一个合理的行为，因为即使原子弹使战争骤然停止，但其目的毕竟是杀死无辜平民。

创作背景

与安斯康姆文章最相关的社会因素或许是第二次世界大战后英国的社会进步主义*。进步主义倾向于取消长久以来存在的道德禁律，例如反对通过轰炸平民来缩短战争时间的规则。这样做的理由是，通过取消这些规则的限制，全世界总体的苦难将被最小化，而全世界总体的福祉将被最大化。安斯康姆在其广播讲话《牛津大学的道德哲学有没有让年轻人堕落？》[3]中提到这种观点，她坚信有些行为本身就是绝对错误的。

　　这种立场使安斯康姆成为一个道德绝对论者。她认为牛津大学的道德哲学并非让年轻人堕落的罪魁祸首——牛津大学的道德哲学只是当时进步主义社会思潮的反映而已："这种哲学完全是从时代精神中孕育而生的，或许可被称为时代精神的谄媚哲学。"[4] 安斯康姆对进步论的批评是基于她认为的道德哲学的目的：教会学生去质疑流行的伦理思潮。而她认为这一点是她的同事们完全没有做到的。

1. G. E. M. 安斯康姆："现代道德哲学"，《哲学》第 33 卷，1958 年第 124 期，第 1—19 页。

2. 参见 G. E. M. 安斯康姆："现代道德哲学"；安斯康姆：《意向》，牛津：布莱克维尔出版社，1957 年；安斯康姆：《因果关系与决定：就职演讲》，剑桥：剑桥大学出版社，1971 年。

3. G. E. M. 安斯康姆："牛津大学的道德哲学有没有让年轻人堕落？"，载《人类生活、行为和伦理学》，圣安德鲁斯哲学和公共政策研究，玛丽·吉奇和卢克·高莫里编，埃克塞特：学术印记出版社，2005 年，Kindle 版；最初发表在《聆听者》第 57 卷，1957 年 2 月 14 日，第 266—267、271 页。文章标题指涉古雅典哲学家苏格拉底，苏格拉底被指控"腐蚀青年"而被处死，事实上，他只是训练年轻人质疑当时流行的文化观念而已。

4. G. E. M. 安斯康姆："牛津大学的道德哲学有没有让年轻人堕落？"，Kindle 版。

2 学术背景

要点 🔑

- 道德哲学关注什么样的事件是道德的，以及如何使用"正确"和"错误"等术语。

- 道德哲学有四大分支：后果论，只关注行为的后果；康德伦理学，关注个人如何确立自己的道德准则；神圣律令伦理学*，关注对上帝律令的遵守；德性伦理学，关注对德性*的理解和培养。

- 安斯康姆认为后果论存在严重的道德问题。她倡导回归心理学支撑下的亚里士多德伦理观*。

著作语境

G. E. M. 安斯康姆在《现代道德哲学》中审视并批判了20世纪50年代主要的道德哲学。

道德哲学探讨道德责任（个体实施或不实施某种行为的要求）的本质、正确的行为，以及善的生活等主题。生活的目的是什么？"后果论"（安斯康姆发明的术语）是这样一种观点，即就道德而言，唯有后果重要。换言之，除非规则、禁令或上帝律令能够促成好的后果，否则毫无意义。但是在这种情况下，是后果，而非规则或律令，使得行为成为道德上好的行为。后果论的一个分支是功利主义*，后者认为唯有产生快乐、减少痛苦才能让行为合乎道德。

后果论之外最重要的当代道德哲学是康德伦理学，这一道德哲学源自18世纪德国哲学家伊曼努尔·康德的思想。康德强调义务，即那些因其本身，而非因其结果而需要遵守的标准或规则；对他来说，义务是任何行为的道德基础。

神圣律法伦理学是这样一种道德观，它认为存在某种神圣旨意来制定我们必须遵守的规则；这也是基督教道德伦理观。

最后，德性伦理学是古典社会最受推崇的道德观。古希腊罗马哲学家认为，伦理学的目的是培养和践行德性（通过人类行为表达出来的人格倾向——例如克制、睿智、勇敢）。

> "《现代道德哲学》同时触及了一些哲学家敏感的神经，他们奉行被她批判的某种观点。部分原因是她在一些批评之中采用了比较严厉的谴责性的或说教性的口吻。"
>
> —— 茱莉亚·德里弗："格特鲁德·伊丽莎白·玛格丽特·安斯康姆"，
> 见《斯坦福哲学百科全书》

学科概览

后果论（通常被称为功利主义）是英国哲学家和社会改革家杰里米·边沁 * 提出的一种著名的思想。他在 1789 年的《道德与立法原理导论》[1] 一书中，提出了一个著名的观点：快乐和痛苦是人类的两个互相竞争的主人——它们"支配着我们所做、所说、所想的一切"。[2] 边沁同时主张，我们应该建立一种计算方法，根据行为带来的快乐的多少，和避免或减轻的痛苦的多少，来确定行为的道德属性。边沁的学生、哲学家约翰·斯图亚特·穆勒 * 在其 1861 年的著作《功利主义》中进一步发展了这一理论。

根据康德伦理学的创始人伊曼努尔·康德的观点，个体根据任何理性的人在特定环境下的共同反应，为自己的道德标准"立法"。这就是所谓的"绝对命令"。举例而言，康德（以及后来的"康德派哲学家"）相信，一个理性的人会选择永不撒谎。这是因为，如果我为了骗取你的钱财而撒了谎，那么我就是在暗中支持他人为了自己的经济利益向我撒谎。这样我就会失去分辨真实和谬误的能力，从而生活在一种自相矛盾、模糊难辨的状态中——这是任何具备理性思考能力的人都不会选择的。

希腊哲学家亚里士多德是德性伦理学最重要的人物。作为影响深远的《尼各马可伦理学》的作者，亚里士多德认为善的生活的根本特征在于某种特定的幸福，叫做"eudaimonia"（希腊语，意指幸福）。幸福是人类最终极的善，为了实现它，我们需要完善诸如勇气、睿智、节制等德性。但亚里士多德的德性伦理学并非将"善"定义为一种精神状态。相反，"正确行为"才是亚里士多德信仰"善行"的关键。[3]

学术渊源

安斯康姆无疑受到了 20 世纪哲学家路德维希·维特根斯坦的启发，维特根斯坦当时对牛津大学和剑桥大学的哲学思想产生了巨大的影响。安斯康姆是他的研究生，她还将他的《哲学研究》翻译成英文。[4]维特根斯坦影响了安斯康姆对"应该"和"责任"等概念的批判。他有一句著名的论断："词语的意义在于它在语言中的使用。"[5]安斯康姆不断质疑"责任"和"应该"等道德术语在日常使用中的含义，因为这些术语总是指向神圣立法者（上帝）的律法。

尽管维特根斯坦在哲学方法论和语言分析方面影响了安斯康姆，但在道德哲学领域对她产生最重要影响的则可能是亚里士多德。在此文中，安斯康姆将所有形式的现代道德哲学同亚里士多德的道德哲学对立起来，并建议通过复兴一些德性的概念让道德哲学重获统一性，她这样说："或许最终我们能够进一步思考某种德性的概念；有了这样的概念，我认为，我们应该可以开始某种形式的伦理学研究了。"[6]

总而言之，诸如"正义"或"审慎"等内涵丰富的概念将胜任哲学工作，而此一任务在现代哲学中本来由"应该"和"道德错误"等概念承担。

1. 杰里米·边沁：《道德与立法原理导论》，牛津：克拉伦登出版社，1907年。
2. 杰里米·边沁：《道德与立法原理导论》，第1页；转引自茱莉亚·德里弗："功利主义的历史"，《斯坦福哲学百科全书》，2014年冬季版，爱德华·N.扎尔塔编，登录日期2015年10月6日，http://plato.stanford.edu/entries/utilitarianism-history/。
3. 亚里士多德：《尼各马可伦理学》，罗杰·克里斯普编译，剑桥：剑桥大学出版社，2014年，第ix、12页。
4. 路德维希·维特根斯坦：《哲学研究》，英语及德语版，G. E. M. 安斯康姆翻译，牛津：巴泽尔·布莱克维尔出版社，1953年。
5. 路德维希·维特根斯坦：《哲学研究》，第4版，2009年，P.M.S. 哈克和约阿希姆·舒尔特编译，牛津：威利·布莱克维尔出版社，2009年，第43页。
6. G. E. M. 安斯康姆："现代道德哲学"，《哲学》第33卷，1958年第124期，第12—13页。

3 主导命题

要点 🔑

- G. E. M. 安斯康姆的《现代道德哲学》的核心问题是：什么是道德责任的本质和意义？

- 就后果论而言，我们在道德上必须实施任何能带来最好后果的行为；伦理反实在论*认为不存在道德事实或道德责任。

- 安斯康姆认为应该抛弃后果论，因为"道德责任"这一思想是神圣律法概念的残余，而神圣律法早已是人们不再普遍相信的概念。

核心问题

G. E. M. 安斯康姆在《现代道德哲学》中的核心论点是关于道德责任的性质和意义。她以一种挑衅和独特的方式提出这一问题，认为道德责任和道德"应该"在她所处时代的哲学话语中已经毫无意义。安斯康姆强烈反对后果论者对那些她认为道德上极其恶劣的行为的辩护，例如美国总统哈里·S. 杜鲁门在二战末期对日本城市广岛和长崎投放原子弹；后果论者认为对数十万无辜平民的屠杀是完全正当合理的，只要从长远来看，它能挽救更多人的生命。安斯康姆认为这样的思维模式与传统道德观完全不符。

后果论者将道德责任限定在纯粹的后果层面，从而回答什么是道德责任的问题。然而，安斯康姆认为，这种意义上的道德责任在古希腊哲学家亚里士多德的语言或道德哲学中找不到任何相似的概念。她认为，道德责任概念是基督教对神圣立法权威的信仰的残余：因为上帝至高无上的力量、权威和智慧，我们必须依据道德规

16

则行事。但是安斯康姆认为，后果论者并不相信上帝，或他们即使相信上帝，也不相信神圣权威创造了我们的道德责任。因此，后果论者在使用"道德责任"概念时并没有厘清其意义。安斯康姆提出道德哲学家应该摒弃"责任"和"应该"这些基督教道德观的残羹剩饭，转而使用正义和节制等内涵更加丰富的德性概念。

> "我母亲坐下来开始阅读标准的现代伦理学著作，她被惊呆了。这些人共同持有的观点，就是让杜鲁门投掷炸弹，也让那些大学教授支持杜鲁门的观点，是安斯康姆称为'后果论'的观点。"
>
> —— 玛丽·吉奇：《人类生活、行为和伦理学：
> G. E. M. 安斯康姆文集》导读

参与者

安斯康姆的文章聚焦 20 世纪上半叶的道德哲学状况。安斯康姆的两位英国前辈对理解她撰写文章的背景至关重要。

第一位是亨利·西奇威克*，他是维多利亚时代（1837—1901）*英国最重要的哲学家。他在道德哲学领域影响最大的作品是《伦理学方法》（1874），标志着功利主义道德传统（一种道德哲学立场，认为最好的行为是能够带来多数人最大程度的幸福的行为）的顶峰。历史学家认为，西奇威克"为 20 世纪功利主义者和其批评者之间的绝大部分论争确立了论点"。[1] 在那个时代，他是一位卓尔不群的思想家，试图把功利主义和伊曼努尔·康德的道义论*（一种建立在责任意识之上的道德哲学）结合起来，建立一种他称之为道德"直觉主义"*的理论思想。西奇威克认为，虽然我们对自己在特定情形下的责任有一定的直觉，但这些关于道德的直觉最终会转化为功利主义的原则。因此，一个人会依照直觉知道不应该在大街上攻击一个无辜的陌生人，但让这一行为成为错误行为的终极原则，却是预防痛苦的功利主义原则。据此推理，一旦发现攻击陌生人可以最终带来好的结果，那么不该攻击陌生人的原则就可以被推翻。

第二位重要的前辈是英国哲学家 G. E. 摩尔*，他继承了西奇威克对直觉主义和功利主义的结合。摩尔是一位极具影响力的思想家，剑桥大学三一学院的教授，著有长篇巨著《伦理学原理》（1903）。在《伦理学原理》中，他提出"善"并非自然属性——将"善"与其他自然之物等量齐观是犯了"自然主义谬误"*。换言之，任何特定的自然之物或自然事实是善是恶始终是一个有待讨论的问题。摩尔得出论断，作为属性的善不能独立于自然之物或事件属性而存在。换言之，善的属性，就如同红色的属性一样：虽然红色可以在特定物体上因该物体的物理属性而被发现，但红色与这些物理属性却截然不同。

这两位哲学家在两个方面奠定了安斯康姆时代道德哲学的基础。第一，他们信奉某种形式的后果论。第二，他们在世界的自然事实和"应该""正确""责任"等概念之间划清界限。对他们来说，没有任何日常事实——例如"孩子口渴了"——包含了任何特定的道德命令，例如"我应该给小孩水喝"。

当代论战

1958 年，为了在牛津大学开设道德哲学课程，安斯康姆梳理了现代道德哲学。她的梳理似乎始于 18 世纪苏格兰哲学家大卫·休谟*和伊曼纽尔·康德，继之以西奇威克、摩尔和她同时代的哲学家。所有这些哲学家都倾向于把"道德"领域和"自然"领域完全分开。休谟认为在"存在"表述和"应该"表述之间没有任何逻辑关联。譬如,事实表述"上帝令你尊重父母"并不推导出道德表述"你应尊重父母",因为两者之间还存在一个并未言明的前提:"你应遵循上帝的任何指令。"

这一没有言明的前提已经包含了"应该",因此已经是一个道德表述,而不是事实表述。休谟指出,在事实的常规世界和"道德必须"的特殊世界之间存在一条鸿沟。[2]

在这种背景之下,安斯康姆将怀疑的目光投向所有这些思想者,并将她从路德维希·维特根斯坦那里学来的语言分析应用到他们的道德哲学中。她这样总结:如果"必须"和"责任"等术语因其与上帝的联系而获得意义,那么它们也因失去了与上帝的联系而丧失意义。

---

1. 巴顿·舒尔茨:"亨利·西奇威克",《斯坦福哲学百科全书》,2015 年夏季版,爱德华·N.扎尔塔编,登录日期 2015 年 10 月 7 日,http://plato.stanford.edu/archives/sum2015/entries/sidgwick/。

2. 大卫·休谟:《人性论》,L. A. 塞尔比-比格和 P. H. 尼迪奇编,第 2 版,牛津:牛津大学出版社,1978 年,第 469—470 页。

4 作者贡献

要点 ⚷━

- 安斯康姆认为道德责任是建立在神圣权威之上的道德体系的残余，而人们已经不再相信神圣权威，因此这一概念应该被摒弃。

- 如此，便为德性伦理学铺平了道路，德性伦理学可以替代后果论，聚焦正义和节制等美德。

- 安斯康姆受到哲学家维特根斯坦的语言分析的影响，并将语言分析应用于道德责任概念。

作者目标

G. E. M. 安斯康姆的《现代道德哲学》的开创性意义在于她提出，当下流行的"应该""责任""正确与错误"和"义务"等术语的"道德"涵义缺乏内在统一性，甚至可以说是毫无必要。这种"道德"涵义并不存在于古希腊哲学家亚里士多德的著作当中，他关注勇气、正义、睿智和节制等德性的属性及其在塑造人类善的生活方面所发挥的作用。亚里士多德著作中缺乏道德责任概念，这表明一种系统的伦理学理论并不需要这样的概念。

安斯康姆认为，道德责任概念缺乏内在统一性。她提出了一种假设，即道德责任概念是亚里士多德和 20 世纪之间两千多年的基督教时期的副产品。她认为，道德责任的意义取决于对神圣立法者（上帝）的信仰，因为无论制定"法律"，还是执行"责任"，都需要一个高高在上的权力和权威。例如，"土地法律"能够发挥作用，是因为整个国家在确保其得以实施，一旦违背，就会被国家机器施以惩罚。安斯康姆似乎表明，上帝和道德责任之间也存在相似的联系。这就给道德哲学家提供了一种选择：要么回到宗教的伦理学观念，要么摒弃"应该"和"责任"等术语，转而使用"正义""德性""罪恶"等内涵更加丰富的概念。这种思想史无前例。

> "首先……我们目前并不适合从事道德哲学研究……第二……责任和义务——**道德**责任和**道德**义务——的概念，也就是说……如果在心理学上可行的话，应该被摒弃……第三……从西奇威克以来的英国著名的道德哲学家之间的差别微乎其微。"
>
> —— G. E. M. 安斯康姆："现代道德哲学"

研究方法

安斯康姆的《现代道德哲学》具有哲学的和公众的双重目的。从哲学意义上来说，此文既采用了强调语言和定义的分析方法，同时也采用了历史方法。她不仅对"应该"等术语的意义提出质疑，而且尽力厘清众多的道德概念。她用亚里士多德的道德哲学来反驳现代哲学家，她写道："任何读过亚里士多德的《伦理学》，同时还读过现代道德哲学的人，都会深刻地感受到两者之间巨大的差异。"[1]虽然在道德哲学研究中使用历史方法并不新奇，但安斯康姆的创新之处在于将亚里士多德的思想用于分析现代道德问题。

安斯康姆还有更广泛的担忧，尤其是她所认为的公民社会普遍的道德滑坡。她认为，这种道德滑坡源自后果论，因为后果论认为，只要基于预见结果，不管看起来如何不道德的行为，都是可以允许的。安斯康姆在文章《杜鲁门先生的学位》（1958）[2]中认为，美国总统哈里·S.杜鲁门批准对日本城市广岛和长崎投放原子弹，从而犯下了大屠杀罪。同样，她在《牛津大学的道德哲学有没有让年轻人堕落？》（1957）中提出，后果论已经导致了一种鼓励压迫的思维模式："预防性措施意味着他们想进入人们的家庭，把他们随意推搡，并非因为他们已经'做了什么'，而仅仅是预防他们万一会做什么。"[3]

她对后果论的担心很显然已经超越了哲学的范畴，而进入了充满问题的公共道德领域。

时代贡献

安斯康姆无疑受到哲学家路德维希·维特根斯坦的影响，有时候她被称为他的弟子。[4]她的研究使用当时非常流行的"日常语言"方法，该方法在一定程度上可以追溯到维特根斯坦，他似乎相信，我们使用语言的方式最终赋予语言以意义。

安斯康姆将这一想法运用在以下方面。

首先，"责任"和"道德应该"等概念从本质上而言，来自犹太教和基督教神学，然后在基督教的框架内被改造为西方哲学的概念。安斯康姆认为，这些术语因为在使用时与上帝相联系而获得意义。然而，当人们放弃了上帝的概念之后，"道德责任"被应用于何种意义就变得晦暗不明了。我们可以在安斯康姆对哲学家伊曼努尔·康德的"绝对命令"*的讨论中发现她的这种思想；对康德来说，我们必须做正确的事情，是因为我们能够为自己立法。而在安斯康姆看来，康德仅仅借用了一个已有的术语，而这一术语的使用只有在与上帝的联系中才具备意义；康德对此一术语的使用让其丧失了所有意义。

1. G. E. M. 安斯康姆："现代道德哲学"，《哲学》第 33 卷，1958 年第 124 期，第 1 页。

2. G. E. M. 安斯康姆："杜鲁门先生的学位"，载《理论学、宗教和政治》，牛津：巴泽尔·布莱克维尔出版社，1981 年。

3. G. E. M. 安斯康姆："牛津大学的道德哲学有没有让年轻人堕落？"，载《人类生活、行为和伦理学》，圣安德鲁斯哲学和公共政策研究，玛丽·吉奇和卢克·高莫里编，埃克塞特：学术印记出版社，2005 年，Kindle 版。

4. 彼得·J. 康拉迪：《艾丽丝·默多克传记》，伦敦：哈珀柯林斯出版社，2002 年，第 266 页："因为［艾丽丝·默多克］出生的时间太晚，而无法听到维特根斯坦讲授的课程，他对她的影响主要通过其弟子如伊丽莎白·安斯康姆来实现。"

第二部分：学术思想

5 思想主脉

要点

- 安斯康姆讨论的要点包括后果论、来自哲学家伊曼努尔·康德思想的伦理哲学（康德伦理学）、道德责任、伦理学的律法概念 *、亚里士多德的伦理观，以及各种德性。

- 她认为，所有的现代道德哲学都在使用道德责任概念，但如果缺乏对制定道德律令的上帝的信仰，那么这一概念就变得毫无意义。

- 安斯康姆认为，所有现代道德哲学在本质上都是一样的，都属于后果论的范畴。她认为，后果论不仅在概念上混淆不清，而且因其支持不道德行为而在道德上也极为危险。

核心主题

G. E. M. 安斯康姆的文章《现代道德哲学》主要有四大论点：

- 可理解性问题：在不相信上帝的情况下，道德哲学家当前对"道德应该""正确""错误"和"义务"等概念的使用在何种意义上可以被人理解？

- 一种有说服力的道德理论必须有内在的一致性，且不是不道德的。

- 后果论、康德主义和契约主义 * 都在某种程度上不符合上述两个标准。

- 在古希腊哲学家亚里士多德的德性伦理学和 18 世纪以来形成的所有道德哲学的伦理学理论之间存在着巨大的分歧。

以上论点综合起来，形成了一条单一的、深刻的、多层次的

问题：对那些拒绝相信上帝的现代哲学家来说，"应该""正确"和
"责任"等道德概念的意义到底是什么？她认为，可能的答案有：
第一，社会意志为"责任"提供了基础；第二，自我立法（自我制
定并遵守的"法律"）为其提供基础；第三，后果为其提供基础。

　　安斯康姆认为，所有这些答案，要么因为缺乏内在一致性而无
法作为"应该"等术语的意义基础，要么在道德上令人无法接受。
相反，她考察了亚里士多德的德性伦理学，这是一种建立在对"睿
智""勇气""正义""真实""节制"等内涵丰富或"稠密"的价值
观和概念的遵守之上的思想，这些价值观和概念既不需要"应该"
和"责任"等概念，也不需要一个神圣立法者。安斯康姆认为，道
德哲学家面临二难选择：要么回到对神圣立法者的某种形式的信
仰，并继续使用"应该"等术语，要么遵循亚里士多德的德性伦理
学的某种版本。

> 　　"安斯康姆的论点如下：第一，**对获利的论断**：当前
> 对我们来说从事道德哲学研究无利可图；第二，**对概念的
> 论断**：'道德责任''道德义务''道德正确与错误''应该'
> 等概念在道德意义上应该被摒弃；第三，**对区分性的论断**：
> 西奇威克以来的英国道德哲学家之间的差别微乎其微。"
> 　　　　—— 罗杰·克里斯普："道德哲学是否建立在错误之上？"

思想探究

　　首先，应该说安斯康姆并没有认为不信上帝的人不能使用"道
德责任""应该"等术语。相反，她认为，因为这些概念最初通过
指向上帝律法或上帝律令而获得意义，所以这些不再相信上帝的人
需要阐明这些术语的意义与用法。

安斯康姆进而讨论了对道德责任概念最有说服力的几种解释——康德主义、契约主义、后果论——她发现每一种解释都存在缺陷。

她认为，康德伦理学的根本观点——自我立法的观点——缺乏内在统一性。康德强调作为自身指导性伦理原则的个体的自治性。但是安斯康姆认为，制定法律需要一个更加强大的力量或权威统治一个更加弱小的力量："立法概念要求立法者具备超越他人的权力。"[1] 因此，在政治领域，由议会或国会这样的机构来颁布法律，其颁布的法律会施加给个体，而个体则必须奉行不悖。但是因为个体不可能同时是立法者和立法的对象，所以将其比喻为政治立法并不贴切。

安斯康姆认为契约主义并不令人满意，这并非基于严格的概念原因，而是基于道德原因。契约主义是指任何预设在一个共同体的成员之间存在隐含的契约，并以此作为道德责任基础的道德理论。她认为，如果我们必须遵守大多数人随机选择的任何道德规范，我们就不可避免地去承担极其不公正的责任。譬如，如果明天大多数人决定必须通过禁止跨种族婚姻来保持种族"纯洁"，我们很难想象契约主义者如何能避免将其变成一个强制性道德责任。

最后，安斯康姆在后果论（任何仅通过行为后果来定义行为道德价值的道德哲学）中发现了多个缺陷。她指出，经典后果论者认为，他们对快乐有一个明确的概念；但他们从未明确指出，快乐到底是一种内在感觉，还是与产生这种感觉的原因有内在联系。英语语言就表明了这一点，例如我们把快乐既定义为**感觉**（"我的胳膊上有一种快乐的感觉"），也定义为**行为**（"投掷棒球是我的一个乐趣"）。她进而提出，即使快乐是一种所有快乐行为都共有的内在感受，但仅仅根据其快乐结果来选择行为的做法也会导致灾难性的道德后果。

为了证明这点，安斯康姆认为，蓄意惩罚无辜者可以是非正义行为的典型。但后果论并不能事先决定惩罚无辜者这样的非正义行为的道德判断：如果一个法官知道判处一个无辜者死刑——因为某种原因——将会挽救其他数个无辜者的生命，那么这一后果表明法官在道德上必须判处该无辜者死刑。

她提出，神圣律法伦理学和亚里士多德伦理学都认为，错误的行为是非正义的，而后果论者总是承认在特定情形下做出非正义行为是正确的。

语言表述

安斯康姆是 20 世纪最伟大的分析哲学家之一，她使用一种以详尽的概念和语言分析为特征的哲学方法。[2] 因此优秀的读者在阅读此文的时候，将会同时关注其细致分析和道德洞见。对同时代读者或非哲学家来说，安斯康姆的用词方式显得有点与众不同。比如，"现代"大致描述了从 17 世纪一直到她所在时代的哲学家——这是一个比通常意义上的"现代"更加宽泛的范畴。

安斯康姆在《现代道德哲学》中创造了术语"后果论"；这一术语后来成了最常见的道德理论术语，用以指称那些将行为的正当性全部建立在其后果之上的道德理论。她同时重新引进了对术语"德性"的哲学用法；德性伦理学或亚里士多德主义现在被认为是可以替代康德主义和后果论的一种思想。

安斯康姆这篇文章的目标读者是哲学研究者，而不是普通读者，而她的文章《牛津大学的道德哲学有没有让年轻人堕落？》表达了与《现代道德哲学》相似的观点，其针对的是更加大众化的读者。安斯康姆的文章以内容晦涩著称。她的女儿曾这样评论："她的文风晦涩而不重复，有时候很难判断应该阅读下一句话，还是回到上一句话，才能搞懂她在说什么。"[3] 但安斯康姆的思想非常系统缜密，行文中会对术语和概念进行定义，当她使用专业语言或例证的时候，并不是为了模糊她所表达的意义，而是为了阐明它。

---

1. G. E. M. 安斯康姆："现代道德哲学"，《哲学》第 33 卷，1958 年第 124 期，第 2 页。
2. 彼得·J. 康拉迪：《艾丽丝·默多克传记》，伦敦：哈珀柯林斯出版社，2002 年，第 283 页："作为她同时代最杰出的英国哲学家，伊丽莎白·安斯康姆从 1946 年起在萨默维尔学院任科研人员。"
3. 玛丽·吉奇："序言"，载 G. E. M. 安斯康姆："牛津大学的道德哲学有没有让年轻人堕落？"，载《人类生活、行为和伦理学》，圣安德鲁斯哲学和公共政策研究，玛丽·吉奇和卢克·高莫里编，埃克塞特：学术印记出版社，2005 年，Kindle 版。

6 思想支脉

要点 🔑

- 《现代道德哲学》有四条主要的思想支脉，共同构成了安斯康姆反对后果论的核心观点。

- 她从德性伦理学——一种借鉴了古希腊哲学家亚里士多德的伦理学的道德哲学思想——的新视角来建构自己的反对意见。

- 安斯康姆对意图的描写和对行为的表述对行为理论——分析人类行为的本质，探讨思维、决定论*和自由意志的哲学分支——产生了重大的影响。

其他思想

G. E. M. 安斯康姆的《现代道德哲学》有四个次要主题：

- 预见后果和蓄意后果之间的差别。
- "需要某种描述的"蓄意行为的概念。
- "应该"和"存在"之间的关系。
- 回归"德性""正义"和"真实"等内涵丰富的伦理学概念，而反对"错误""应该"等笼统的道德概念。

安斯康姆在讨论第一个主题的时候指出，英国哲学家亨利·西奇威克等后果论者坚持一种完全通过行为后果来判断行为道德价值的道德哲学，他们认为所有**预见**后果都是**蓄意**后果。安斯康姆这样总结道：西奇威克"对意图的定义表明个体肯定是计划了他的自愿行为所带来的任何预见性后果"[1]。而安斯康姆认为，一些预见性后果并非蓄意后果。

第二个与其相关联的论点是关于一个行为是否"在特定条件下属于蓄意"。安斯康姆的这一表述在本质上指一个行为作为非正义或谋杀或冷酷无情的行为既是蓄意的，也是计划之内的。也就是说，不仅此行为是有意为之，而且行为人将一切相关因素都纳入了其对此行为的考虑之中。

18世纪苏格兰哲学家大卫·休谟提出，"存在"并不能推导出"应该"，安斯康姆认为，事实情况并非如此简单，并且要判断一个行为是否不正义或冷酷无情，要比判断其是否"在道德上错误"要容易得多。从德性伦理学的角度来说，在特定的情况下，判断一个行为是否冷酷无情，则要相对容易一些。

> "一个人需要为自己的不良行为的不良后果负责，而他不会因为自己的善行而被称颂；反之，他不需要为自己的善行的不良后果负责。"
>
> ——G. E. M. 安斯康姆："现代道德哲学"

思想探究

后果论者认为，在选择行动（或不行动）的时候，具有导致特定预期后果的意图，还是具有导致同样预期后果的**可能性**，两者之间并无差别。

安斯康姆反对这样的立场，她举例来说明自己的观点：一个人是一个小孩的唯一抚养人，他必须在两种行为之间进行选择。他要么必须实施一些与其毫无关系的非正义行为（诸如为一个腐败官僚盗窃公共资金），从而面临判刑入狱的威胁，要么拒绝参与腐败行为，从而被官僚关入监狱，继而丧失抚养小孩的能力。根据后果论观点，他必须在蓄意放弃抚养小孩（因为，对后果论而言，所有预见后果都是蓄意后果）的"罪恶"和蓄意实施非正义行为的罪恶之间进行权衡。

即使这种非正义行为是罪恶的，后果论者也会认为此人选择这样做是合情合理的，因为这样的话，他就不会丧失对小孩的抚养。安斯康姆认为这是一个问题："一个人需要为自己不良行为的不良后果负责，但他不会因为自己的善行而被称颂；反之，他不需要为自己的善行的不良后果负责。"[2]

安斯康姆进而讨论了她称之为"需要描述的"蓄意行为。她以此来表示一个没有得到充分描述或解释的行为有可能在道德上被误解。譬如，破坏他人的房屋通常情况下被认为是非正义的。但如果你破坏房屋的目的是防止火灾从一个村庄蔓延到另一个村庄，那么这一情形将会改变我们对这种行为的道德判断。

然而，后果论者则会认为，在这种情形下，是**后果**使得这样一个非正义行为在道德上变得正确（当然，这个案例中，拯救了其他的房屋）。但对安斯康姆来说，意图至关重要。她认为，对此一行为详细的描述将会表明后果论者所谓的非正义行为因为其预期结果而变得道德是不正确的[3]：为了防止火灾蔓延而烧毁一间房屋并不能被准确地描述为"非正义行为"或"纵火"。

正如我们所见，大卫·休谟将"存在"和"应该"截然分开。安斯康姆认为，很多一般事实描述隐含了责任——换种说法，某种"应该"已经包含在这一"存在"中了。如果我欠别人钱，就"应该"偿还债务。因此，如果肉店送肉上门，我就欠了钱，从而应该偿还。换句话说，对正义的分析表明，我们**能够**从"存在"中得出"应该"。在关于相互关系和机制的事实表述中，往往包含着确定某一正义行为的必要信息。

最后，安斯康姆重新使用了建立在德性伦理学之上的诸如正义和冷酷无情等内涵丰富的概念，来替代"应该"和"正确"等概念。比方说，因为有了小孩而无法出国度假从而选择堕胎是一个冷酷无情罪恶的例证，但为了挽救母亲的生命而选择堕胎则不能被称为冷酷无情，这一判断无关其他任何伦理考量。[4]这里她和后果论者直接对立，对后果论者而言，只要某一行为能够导致可以预见的最好的后果，即使这一行为是冷酷无情的，它也是可以被允许的。

被忽视之处

作为一篇非常有名而相对简明的文章，《现代道德哲学》已经得到了充分的研究、批评和阐释。然而，文中依然有一个相当简略的评述需要进一步探讨。

安斯康姆反对伊曼努尔·康德的道德哲学立场，因为其要求"自我立法"的概念，而这一概念在她看来是荒诞无稽的。[5]她在写作此文的时候，维特根斯坦对遵循规则和非指涉性语言使用的分析，即"日常语言"哲学，在牛津大学和剑桥大学成为热门话题；安斯康姆应该对这些思想非常熟悉。而康德伦理学在当时鲜有追随者。

自《现代道德哲学》发表之后，人们对康德伦理学产生了新的兴趣。例如，美国德性伦理学家约翰·罗尔斯*极具影响力的一部专著《正义论》（1971）[6]就让康德重新获得关注，从而让安斯康姆对康德的反对观点为更多的读者所熟知。另外一个学者在其研究安斯康姆哲学的专著中辟专章讨论道德的法律概念。[7]安斯康姆自己也撰写了一篇后续文章——《规则、权力和承诺》[8]，以进一步探讨责任的本质和遵循规则等思想。

---

1. G. E. M. 安斯康姆："现代道德哲学"，《哲学》第 33 卷，1958 年第 124 期，第 9 页。

2. 安斯康姆："现代道德哲学"，第 10 页。

3. 安斯康姆："现代道德哲学"，第 13 页。

4. 对这一思想的发展，参见罗莎琳德·赫斯特豪斯："德性理论和堕胎"，《哲学与公共事务》第 20 卷，1999 年第 3 期，第 238—242 页。

5. 安斯康姆："现代道德哲学"，第 2 页。

6. 约翰·罗尔斯：《正义论》，麻省剑桥：哈佛大学出版社，1971 年。

7. 罗杰·泰克曼：《伊丽莎白·安斯康姆的哲学》，牛津：牛津大学出版社，2008 年。

8. G. E. M. 安斯康姆："规则、权力和承诺"，载《伦理学、宗教和政治》，牛津：巴泽尔·布莱克维尔出版社，1981 年。

7 历史成就

要点 🔑

- 安斯康姆对后果论提出质疑，并在道德哲学领域提出一个新的概念：德性伦理学。

- 德性伦理学可以很有效地在政府决策和医学伦理学*领域发挥作用。

- 安斯康姆的基督教信仰或许限制了文章的影响力；有人认为此文是在隐性传教，从而认为其缺乏价值。

观点评价

G. E. M. 安斯康姆在《现代道德哲学》中试图革新她的整个研究领域。她的目的有三：证明"除非我们具备充分的心理哲学，当前很显然我们在这方面非常欠缺"，[1] 否则我们无法从事道德哲学研究；表明如果缺乏对道德规范的神圣立法者的信仰，"道德责任"和"应该"等概念就不可避免地存在问题；证明此前 75 年间大多数英国道德哲学家在本质上都是一样的——他们都拒绝基督教，转而接受后果论。

这篇文章雄心勃勃，但也的确在一定程度上实现了她的目标。她成功地对后果论和康德伦理学的概念基础和道德基础进行了尖锐的批判。文章的影响是立竿见影的，很多道德哲学家因此放弃了后果论。[2] 她还揭示出在亚里士多德的道德哲学和现代道德哲学之间存在的巨大差异，从而重新引发了对德性伦理学的兴趣。安斯康姆用极其吸引人和有意思的方式论证自己对德性的青睐，而这一点激励了其他的哲学家来追随她的脚步。

> "《现代道德哲学》引发了对将德性作为道德思想所需的核心概念的回归。此文影响巨大，先是让她在牛津的大部分同事，后来或许让全世界的大多数哲学家，都反对把功利主义作为一种道德和政治理论。"

> —— 西蒙·布莱克本："反对安斯康姆"，《泰晤士报文学增刊》

当时的成就

虽然 G. E. M. 安斯康姆的《现代道德哲学》主要是一篇哲学论文，但它与当时的政治和社会思潮也有着直接的关联。第二次世界大战中，德国的德雷斯顿等城市遭到了狂轰滥炸，导致交战双方大量的平民伤亡。此举引发了新的道德问题，因为"全面战争"的思维模式意味着国家可以将屠杀平民作为结束战争的手段。安斯康姆对此震惊万分，从而开始思考这样不道德的想法是如何产生的。她的结论是，自维多利亚时代哲学家亨利·西奇威克到她所在时代的所有英国道德哲学家都在为这种不道德的想法辩护。因此，安斯康姆的观点——蓄意杀害无辜平民等行为永远不能得到支持，无论所谓的好处是什么——在她所在的时代是非常激进的。因此，一些人认为安斯康姆秉持一种极端的道德立场。[3]

安斯康姆是几代人中最早提出道德哲学应该回归德性伦理学的哲学家之一，因此，可以说她是一位具有革命性的人物。这也意味着她的文章在发表之初被人轻视。但因为她的思想与同时代的其他道德哲学家的思想大相径庭，所以她的思想给人以新奇感，并逐渐得到支持。

局限性

《现代道德哲学》的局限之一，或许是文章主要聚焦安斯康姆同时代的哲学家及他们的道德哲学立场。这些哲学家包括 R.M. 黑尔*和帕特里克·诺埃尔-史密斯*。她批评他们从本质上来说缺乏独创性，认为他们及其前辈之间的差别"微乎其微"。[4]虽然安斯康姆主要挑战那些如今大多已被世人遗忘的哲学家，但她也囊括了哲学史上几位重要的道德哲学家。

因此，尽管她对后果论哲学家之间相似性的讨论显得有点过时，但她文中有两点却具有普遍的适用性。第一点是对道德概念和道德责任与假设的神圣立法权威之间的关系的全面分析。第二点是对后果论的伦理立场和以德性为基础的伦理立场的对比分析。

挑剔的读者会指出安斯康姆的文章对宗教和道德哲学的关系语焉不详。有些哲学家认为安斯康姆在宣称无神论者无法有意义地使用道德概念，从而让他们心生反感，故而将此文搁置一边。例如，英国哲学家西蒙·布莱克本*如此写道："如果我感觉我必须避免使用［'应该'和'责任'等术语］，因为我被告知这些术语是那些相信神圣律法的人的专有特权，那么我就是受到了欺骗和掠夺。"[5]

然而，大部分评论者并不赞同布莱克本的观点。安斯康姆研究者大多认为安斯康姆根本没有反对世俗道德哲学存在的可能性，她只是想帮助世俗哲学家建立一个基于德性而非神学概念之上的道德哲学的概念体系。

---

1. G.E.M. 安斯康姆："现代道德哲学"，《哲学》第 33 卷，1958 年第 124 期，第 1 页。
2. 西蒙·布莱克本："反对安斯康姆：《人类生活、行为和伦理学》书评"，《泰晤

士报文学增刊》，2005 年 9 月 30 日，第 11—12 页。

3. 这一点从以下事实中可见一斑：牛津大学除了安斯康姆，仅仅有 4 位学者投票反对向美国总统哈里·S.杜鲁门授予荣誉学位，而杜鲁门是唯一一个对人类使用原子弹的国家领导。

4. 安斯康姆："现代道德哲学"，第 1 页。

5. 西蒙·布莱克本："《人类生活、行为和伦理学》书评"。

8 著作地位

要点 &—┉

- 安斯康姆的著作兼容并蓄。她翻译了维特根斯坦的《哲学研究》[1]，发表专著《意向》[2]（行为理论的开拓性著作），并凭借文章《现代道德哲学》开创了德性伦理学这一领域。

- 《现代道德哲学》就其影响力而言，或许只有《意向》能够与其相提并论。

- 虽然很多人知道安斯康姆主要是因为她是维特根斯坦的翻译者，但《现代道德哲学》使得安斯康姆自身成为一位著名的哲学家。

定位

G. E. M. 安斯康姆的《现代道德哲学》发表于 1958 年，当时她正处于哲学事业的巅峰。她此前已经发表了研究不同问题的文章，在英国哲学界地位显著。1953 年，安斯康姆翻译了维特根斯坦去世后发表的《哲学研究》，这是一部非常重要的译著，维特根斯坦或许一直是对她的思想影响最大的人物。但安斯康姆关于道德哲学的研究基本上从 1957—1958 年才全力展开。

1957 年，安斯康姆发表广播讲话《牛津大学的道德哲学有没有让年轻人堕落？》，在讲话中她谴责了牛津大学教授道德哲学的方式。次年，她发表的《现代道德哲学》是她对缺乏内在一致性的当代道德体系所做出的哲学回应。

同样在 1958 年，安斯康姆出版了一本重要的小册子《杜鲁门先生的学位》[3]，批评了美国总统哈里·S.杜鲁门对日本城市广岛和长崎的平民进行的轰炸，同时也批评了牛津大学随后授予其荣誉学位的决定。事实上，安斯康姆的好几篇作品都在某种程度上与第二次世界大战及其战后形势相关。她的第一部出版物——《当前战争的正义性考察》[4]——写于1939年，讨论第二次世界大战的道德主题。毫不夸张地说，盟军（由美国和英国领导的军队）在二战中轰炸平民百姓、要求无条件投降等政策，是导致安斯康姆反思道德哲学的最主要的原因。她1971年的演讲《因果关系与决定》[5]，在哲学领域也具有重要的影响。

> "伊丽莎白·安斯康姆被广泛认为是维特根斯坦最出色的学生，同时为他的作品提供了绝佳的翻译和诠释。她本人也是一位有独到见解、令人敬畏的哲学家，很显然她能够将其虔诚的罗马天主教信仰同她从弗雷格、亚里士多德或维特根斯坦本人那里学到的东西相调和。"
>
> —— 西蒙·布莱克本："反对安斯康姆"，《泰晤士报文学增刊》

整合

安斯康姆一生的作品都聚焦人类行为的分析。她用专业细节探讨什么是"有意"为之，并于1957年写作《意向》来讨论这一问题。这本著作时至今日依然被视为20世纪的哲学经典，在学术文章和专著中被引用超过3 000次。《现代道德哲学》也属于安斯康姆对我们"应该"如何行动的哲学——道德责任（要求个体做什么或不做什么）——的整体探索。

安斯康姆在罗马天主教的基督教道德观领域的写作同样不可忽视。她的文章《避孕和贞洁》[6]和《行为、意图和"双重效应"》[7]在天主教徒和其他读者中影响深远。然而，安斯康姆的天主教思想和她的道德哲学之间并没有真正的界限。比如，她在关于天主教道德神学的文章《当前战争的正义性考察》中表达了对当时人们不再信仰自然道德法则的担忧。这一思想很显然是她在《现代道德哲学》中所表达的思想的先声，她在《现代道德哲学》中认为，道德责任因为人们拒绝信仰基督教而丧失了其意义内涵。

意义

《现代道德哲学》一文是安斯康姆最有影响力的道德哲学著作。或许只有她的专著《意向》堪与其比肩。后者发表时间稍早，并且首次使安斯康姆作为思想家而声名鹊起。

作为 20 世纪道德哲学领域最重要的作品之一，安斯康姆的文章主要在两个领域做出了贡献。首先，她在道德哲学领域发起了德性伦理学运动。德性伦理学强调正义、勇气和睿智等人格素质及其对特定行为的影响。参与这一运动的有菲利帕·富特、阿拉斯戴尔·麦金太尔和罗莎琳德·赫斯特豪斯等颇具影响力的道德哲学家。德性伦理学的学术地位日益显著，如今在道德哲学家中享有广泛的声誉。2013年一部关于德性伦理学运动的完整文选得以出版，学者们将该运动追溯到安斯康姆的这篇文章。[8] 英国道德哲学家安东尼·奥希尔* 如此总结："在一定程度上，在一定范围内，安斯康姆的文章改变了道德哲学，而且在很多人看来，这种改变是向好的。"[9]

第二，安斯康姆的文章引发了人们对道德责任问题和神圣律令伦理学问题的极大兴趣。和安斯康姆一样，神圣律令理论家也认为，上帝和道德责任之间存在必然联系。支持这一观点的著作有美国哲学家菲利普·L. 奎恩* 的《神圣律令和道德要求》[10]，和罗伯特·亚当斯* 的《有限的善和无限的善》[11]。亚当斯影响深远，他提出"责任""有罪""道德应该"等术语从本质上来说都是社会性的，因此的确需要一个我们对其负责的神圣存在。这种立场同《现代道德哲学》的观点非常一致，因为在安斯康姆看来，这些概念的社会性唯有通过上帝才能得以解释。

1. 路德维希·维特根斯坦：《哲学研究》，英语及德语版，G.E.M.安斯康姆译，牛津：巴泽尔·布莱克维尔出版社，1953 年。

2. G.E.M.安斯康姆：《意向》，牛津：牛津大学出版社，1957 年。

3. G.E.M.安斯康姆："杜鲁门先生的学位"，载《伦理学、宗教和政治》，牛津：巴泽尔·布莱克维尔出版社，1981 年。

4. G.E.M.安斯康姆："当前战争的正义性考察"，载《伦理学、宗教和政治》，牛津：巴泽尔·布莱克维尔出版社，1981 年。

5. G.E.M.安斯康姆：《因果关系与决定：就职演讲》，剑桥：剑桥大学出版社，1971 年。

6. G.E.M.安斯康姆：《避孕和贞洁》，伦敦：天主教真理社，1975 年。

7. G.E.M.安斯康姆："行为、意图和'双重效应'"，《美国天主教哲学学会会刊》，1982 年第 56 期，第 12—25 页。

8. 丹尼尔·C.拉塞尔编：《剑桥德性伦理学词典》，剑桥：剑桥大学出版社，2013 年，第 5 页。

9. 安东尼·奥希尔："前言"，《现代道德哲学：皇家哲学学院增刊》第 54 卷，安东尼·奥希尔编，剑桥：剑桥大学出版社，2004 年。

10. 菲利普·奎恩：《神圣律令和道德要求》，牛津：克拉伦登逻辑和哲学图书馆，1978 年。

11. 罗伯特·亚当斯：《有限的善和无限的善：伦理学简介》，牛津：牛津大学出版社，2002 年。

第三部分：学术影响

9 最初反响

要点 ⚷

- 《现代道德哲学》的批评者认为：即使没有神圣权威，道德责任也是可能成立的；安斯康姆对后果论的批评并非无懈可击；德性伦理学尚需继续探讨。

- 安斯康姆及其支持者认为，区分预见后果和蓄意后果对阐明道德哲学至关重要；既然德性伦理学并不需要依赖神圣权威而存在，那么它就是一种可行的伦理哲学。

- 安斯康姆后来就人类行为及其预见后果之间的关系问题进行了更加细致的探讨。

批评

对 G. E. M. 安斯康姆的《现代道德哲学》最为广泛的批评之一是，她没有就道德观念取决于上帝信仰的观点进行有说服力的论证。

譬如，哲学家凯·尼尔森*发表过一篇批评安斯康姆的文章，题为《论道德独立于宗教》。[1]他这样说："即使我们知道了上帝的存在以及上帝颁布律法，这本身并不能告诉我们什么是正确的，或者我们应该做什么。"[2]这个问题古希腊哲学家柏拉图*在其作品《欧绪弗洛篇》[3]中进行了讨论，他将其概括为所谓的欧绪弗洛难题：是上帝的命令使一个行为正确，还是上帝因为特定行为本身正确而命令这些行为？如果属于前者，那么上帝有可能命令一些十恶不赦的行为。如果属于后者，那么上帝根本就不是道德规范的基础。尼尔森断言，这一问题"自《欧绪弗洛篇》问世以来"

第三部分 | 9. 最初反响

已经被解决了。[4]

安斯康姆还受到来自后果论者的批评，他们试图为自己的道德理论辩护。例如美国哲学家乔纳森·贝内特＊就提出，安斯康姆对蓄意行为和预见行为的区分与道德评价毫无关系。贝内特列举了医学伦理学的例子，提出杀人和放任死亡在道德上没有本质的区别。[5] 例如，医生如果在有人心跳骤停的时候袖手旁观，那他绝对不能因为他只是"让此人死亡"，而不是杀死此人而获得宽恕。对安斯康姆文章的积极评价主要关注道德哲学领域中德性的重新崛起。

> "即使我们知道了上帝的存在以及上帝颁布律法，这本身并不能告诉我们什么是正确的，或者我们应该做什么。"
>
> —— 凯·尼尔森：《论道德独立于宗教》

回应

不幸的是，虽然有人指责安斯康姆对道德观念依赖宗教而存在的论证缺乏说服力，但她并未对此作出回应。事实上，对于安斯康姆写作此文是否用来隐性支持对上帝的信仰这一说法，评论者中尚存在争议。尽管依然有人认为她有这方面的嫌疑，[6] 但大家似乎都一致认为，隐性传教并非她提出这一论点的首要目的——当然了，不是首要目的并不意味着她不相信其中的关联。哲学家 D.J. 李克特＊就认为："如果我们从［安斯康姆的］讨论中得出结论，认为只有神圣律法或亚里士多德的伦理概念才是有效的，那我们就犯了错误"，因为安斯康姆自己对这两种道德观念进行过讨论，认为两者都有缺陷。[7] 简言之，安斯康姆对道德责任的其他阐释持开放态度；她只是发现所有这些阐释都有严重缺陷而已。

面对《现代道德哲学》受到的批判，安斯康姆最明晰的回应应该来自杂志《分析》中的一条非常简短的说明，她以此说明来回应贝内特对她将行为和后果区分开来的做法的批评。[8]她这样写道："贝内特先生的论证逻辑是这样的，如果你不做B就会导致A，那么你不做B而做的任何事情都导致A。尽管就此可以长篇大论，但这一逻辑看上去似乎就不对。"[9]这次交锋发生时，安斯康姆刚刚开始进行意图与任何道德哲学的相关性的研究。

冲突与共识

尽管安斯康姆似乎一生都在坚持她对后果论的批判，但她的确试图界定出更加清晰的概念，从而更好地对有不良的预见后果却并非蓄意后果的行为进行道德判断。事实上，她的《行为、意图和"双重效应"》[10]就详尽解释了这些概念。安斯康姆认为，如果你预见到修建高速公路几乎必然会导致一些人的死亡，但却没有足够的理由说你"蓄意"让这些预见后果发生——因此不能说你有罪。她似乎在回应贝内特等后果论者对她的指责，例如贝内特对她区分蓄意后果和预见后果十分不屑。贝内特等人这样说的理由是，他们认为安斯康姆仅仅在照搬罗马天主教的双重效应：你不能为了实现其他目标（即使是好的目标）而杀人，但你可以执行某种带有致人死亡的预期副作用的行为。

安斯康姆在《行为、意图和"双重效应"》中回应说，她并非坚持"双重效应"论，而是坚持"副作用原则"，她这样写道："与'副作用原则'相关的是绝对禁止寻求他人死亡，无论将其作为目的还是作为手段……'副作用原则'并未说明你什么时候会导致预期的死亡。"[11] 简言之，安斯康姆关心的**仅仅**是证明，即使明知某一行为会直接致人死亡，但这一行为并非总是错的。她的原则试图表明从活人身上摘取器官给他人移植和修建高速公路之间有所不同。它们都会导致至少一人死亡的预见后果——但在她看来，前者是谋杀，而后者不是。

1. 凯·尼尔森："论道德独立于宗教"，《思想》第70卷，1961年第278期，第175—186页。

2. 凯·尼尔森："论道德独立于宗教"，第175页。

3. 参见柏拉图：《欧绪弗洛篇》，载《古希腊哲学读本》，第2版，S.马克·科恩和帕特丽夏·科德编，C.D.C.里夫翻译，印第安纳波利斯：哈克特出版社，2005年，第97—114页。

4. 凯·尼尔森："论道德独立于宗教"，第175页。

5. 乔纳森·贝内特："无论后果如何"，《分析》第26卷，1966年第2期，第83—102页。

6. 参见托马斯·平克："道德责任"，载《现代道德哲学：皇家哲学学院增刊》第54卷，安东尼·奥希尔编。剑桥：剑桥大学出版社，2004年，第159—169页；和尼尔森："论道德独立于宗教"。

7. D.J.李克特：《安斯康姆之后的伦理学：后〈现代道德哲学〉》，多德雷赫特：斯普林格出版社，2000年，第29页。

8. 乔纳森·贝内特："无论后果如何"。

9. G.E.M.安斯康姆："关于贝内特先生的一条说明"，《分析》第26卷，1966年第6期，第208页。

10. G.E.M.安斯康姆："行为、意图和'双重效应'"，《美国天主教哲学学会会刊》，1982年第56期，第12—25页。

11. 安斯康姆："行为、意图和'双重效应'"。

10 后续争议

要点 🗝

- 德性伦理学正在道德哲学领域蓬勃发展，为寻找替代后果论的理论开辟了一条路径。

- 德性伦理学认为，道德哲学的目的是用心理学、文学和历史来分析睿智和节制等德性。

- 《现代道德哲学》在道德哲学中引进了一个新的分支学科，该分支继续朝着众多的方向发展。

应用与问题

G. E. M. 安斯康姆的《现代道德哲学》对"道德责任"和"道德应该"等概念提出了深刻的质疑。安斯康姆认为，"如果在心理学上可行的话，责任和义务的概念应该被摒弃。"[1]

那些支持康德伦理学和功利主义（安斯康姆为其创造了一个术语"后果论"）的哲学家不赞成这一观点。这两种理论都有赖于"道德责任"的世俗解释，而安斯康姆则在质疑这一概念是否具有意义。

正如哲学家西蒙·布莱克本所承认的那样，此文"影响巨大，先是让她在牛津的大部分同事，后来或许让全世界的大多数哲学家，都反对把功利主义作为一种道德和政治理论"。[2] 其结果是，人们开始研究德性伦理学传统中的道德思想。安斯康姆激发了人们对德性伦理学的普遍兴趣，尤其是对亚里士多德伦理学的兴趣。

> "伊丽莎白·安斯康姆的《现代道德哲学》在所谓的'德性伦理学'的发展中发挥了重大作用，德性伦理学尤其在过去 30 年得到了快速发展。"
>
> —— 罗杰·克里斯普："道德哲学是否建立在一个错误之上？"

思想流派

这一伦理学的新立场在德性伦理学和实验道德心理学领域催生了大量的研究。虽然安斯康姆本人并没有对德性伦理学的概念展开全面的研究，但她的文章鼓励了众多其他的哲学家试图在当代道德哲学中探索出一种运用德性的方法。

安斯康姆的好友和同事、哲学家菲利帕·富特发表《德性与罪恶》[3] 和《自然的善》[4]，这是两部德性伦理学的经典。安斯康姆的丈夫彼得·吉奇也在 1974 年发表了专著《德性论》。富特和吉奇都坚持一种对德性的"自然主义"阐释——即该阐释建立在人类生物学和社会学，而不是"道德责任"的基础之上。例如吉奇有一句名言："人类因德性而受益，如同蜜蜂因蜂针而受益一样。"[5] 换言之，德性是正常人类的正常品质的一部分；如果没有德性，我们就会有缺陷，就无法充分发展。菲利帕·富特在其 2001 年的专著《自然的善》中提出，人类生物特征能够为德性伦理学提供依据。[6]

除了道德哲学领域的德性伦理学运动，安斯康姆的文章还影响了基督教伦理学，或道德神学（"神学"指对宗教概念的系统研究，通常通过对《圣经》的分析来进行）。譬如，神学家斯坦利·哈弗罗斯 * 和威廉·弗兰克纳 * 就在 20 世纪 70 年代开始探讨基督教对德性的阐释。尤其是哈弗罗斯的作品吸收了德性伦理学在基督教神学和生活中的运用。[7]

当代研究

当代德性伦理学运动或许正处在历史上最蓬勃发展的时期；2013年，剑桥大学出版社出版了一部德性伦理学的全集。[8] 安斯康姆的影响不可低估，在当下德性伦理学运动中讨论的诸多问题都可以追溯到她关于德性伦理学的中世纪[*]和古代[*]渊源的著作。

安斯康姆对亚里士多德和中世纪神学家托马斯·阿奎那[*]的伦理学的评述具有非常重要的学术意义。阿拉斯戴尔·麦金太尔是当代德性伦理学领域最重要的学者之一，他的著作《追寻美德》发表于1981年。[9] 在该书中，麦金太尔讨论了安斯康姆的数个主题，其中包括对德性的详尽的概念阐释。[10] 麦金太尔还发表了《依赖性的理性动物》，讨论人类生物学特征对我们思考德性和道德培养的方式的影响。[11]

奥克兰大学的罗莎琳德·赫斯特豪斯是德性伦理学领域的另一位领军人物，她于2001年发表的专著《德性伦理学》是对德性伦理学领域的重大贡献。赫斯特豪斯提出，德性伦理学能够制定她所谓的"v规则"，即建立在德性（virtues）和罪恶（vices）之上的规则。[12] 因此，如果一个人明白，为了职业发展而选择堕胎是一种冷酷无情的行为，那么她就不应该堕胎。这些规则使得德性伦理学成为一种"规范性"道德理论，从而与后果论和康德伦理学相抗衡。

德性伦理学的最新支持者包括玛莎·努斯鲍姆[*]和著名的印度经济学家阿马蒂亚·森[*]。玛莎·努斯鲍姆是一位美国哲学家，主要研究古代哲学和文学。她在道德心理学领域发表了一些重要的作品，强调爱、同情、悲伤、羞愧和厌恶等情绪在道德思考中的重要性。她还和阿马蒂亚·森合作，建构福利经济学的"可行能力"理论，探讨兴旺生活所需的核心能力。努斯鲍姆列举了 10 种能力，其中包括形成情感依恋的能力、推理的能力、玩乐的能力和保持健康的能力。这一理论可用于比较和衡量国际发展，并有助于形成人类发展指数——一种衡量社会发展水平的国际指标。

1. G.E.M.安斯康姆："现代道德哲学"，《哲学》第 33 卷，1958 年第 124 期，第 1 页。
2. 西蒙·布莱克本："反对安斯康姆：《人类生活、行为和伦理学》书评"，《泰晤士报文学增刊》，2005 年 9 月 30 日，第 11—12 页。
3. 菲利帕·富特：《美德与罪恶和道德哲学的其他文章》，伯克利和洛杉矶：加利福尼亚大学出版社，1978 年。
4. 菲利帕·富特：《自然的善》，牛津：牛津大学出版社，2001 年。
5. 彼得·吉奇：《德性论》，剑桥：剑桥大学出版社，1977 年，第 vii 页。
6. 富特：《自然的善》，第 51 页。
7. 斯坦利·哈弗罗斯：《人格与基督教人生》，德克萨斯州圣安东尼奥：三一大学出版社，1975 年。
8. 丹尼尔·C.拉塞尔编：《剑桥德性伦理学词典》，剑桥：剑桥大学出版社，2013 年。
9. 阿拉斯戴尔·麦金太尔：《追寻美德》，第 3 版修订版，伦敦：达克沃斯出版社，2007 年。
10. 麦金太尔：《追寻美德》，第 191 页。
11. 阿拉斯戴尔·麦金太尔：《依赖性的理性动物》，伦敦：达克沃斯出版社，2007 年。
12. 罗莎琳德·赫斯特豪斯：《德性伦理学》，牛津：牛津大学出版社，2001 年，第 36—42 页。

11 当代印迹

要点 ⚷

- 《现代道德哲学》把道德哲学分为后果论、康德伦理学和德性伦理学，从而更加清晰地界定了道德哲学。

- 该文提出的康德伦理学的问题，即康德的自我立法概念——制定并执行自我的"法律"——缺乏内在统一性，时至今日依然有效。

- 安斯康姆认为后果论和康德伦理学都是不道德的。

地位

G. E. M. 安斯康姆的《现代道德哲学》对当代学术争论的一大贡献是创造了"后果论"一词。在她发表此文之前，一大批道德理论都被归纳在"功利主义"（一种道德和政治哲学，根据能否为大多数人带来最大程度的幸福来判断行为）这一术语之下。

她的第二大贡献是对道德责任（对个体做什么或不做什么的要求）概念提出严重的质疑；安斯康姆的观点引发了进一步的研究，例如探讨应该用"自然主义"还是应该用"非自然主义"的术语来理解伦理学。支持自然主义伦理学的人认为，伦理判断和日常价值判断在本质上具有相似之处：如果农民种出好的蔬菜，从而能够维持农场运转，那么他就是一个好农民。非自然主义者认为，在事实和价值之间存在差别，因此"善"或"正确"的品质必然是特定行为的非自然品质。比如，足球使人快乐（对非自然主义者而言），并不能推导出看球赛是道德上正确的行为。你所感受到的快乐必须还要具备"善"的品质。

最后，此文将当代伦理学领域分为三大类：后果论、康德伦理学和德性伦理学。事实上，这篇文章在今天依然在大量的德性伦理学专著和文章中被反复引用，因此对试图理解道德哲学的学生而言，此文是一个重要的起点。

> "伊丽莎白·安斯康姆和菲利帕·富特等哲学家……主张转向德性伦理学，将其视为当代解释和建构伦理学核心概念的逻辑结论。"
>
> —— 丹尼尔·C.拉塞尔主编:《剑桥德性伦理学词典》

互动

《现代道德哲学》在今天依然十分重要，因为它最先对后果论提出了重大批判，其学术深度让其能够倡导一种替代后果论的道德哲学思想。虽然此文对后果论有诸多影响，但其中有三点最为突出。

首先，安斯康姆认为后果论从未绝对禁止任何行为。譬如，因为将无辜者判刑并处死会导致有益的后果，至少这种可能性是存在的，所以一个后果论者从来不会简单地禁止此类不公正行为。

其次，安斯康姆提出了一个很有说服力的观点：虽然后果论，尤其是功利主义形式的后果论，完全建立在"快乐"概念之上，但它甚至无法对快乐的内涵进行充分阐释。因此，今天的后果论者往往关注满足偏好，而不是实现快乐。

第三，关于蓄意后果和纯粹的预见后果之间的区别，今天依然存在很多的争论。安斯康姆在1981年发表的《行为、意图和"双重效应"》中重新讨论了这一问题，对区分蓄意后果和预见后果的重要性进行了详细的辩护。[1]然而，很多后果论者坚持认为，这两者在道德上并不存在显著区别。哲学教授乔纳森·贝内特是最早批评安斯康姆的学者之一，他在《道德与后果》[2]和《行为本身》（1995）[3]中对这一区分做了进一步的探讨。

持续争议

安斯康姆反对"从西奇威克至今"的所有后果论者。[4]澳大利亚哲学家彼得·辛格*是后果论的现代维护者，他在专著《世界观：西奇威克和当代伦理学》中为西奇威克做了系统的辩护。[5]西奇威克在今天依旧具有现实意义——甚至对辛格等最著名的后果论哲学家来说也是如此——表明安斯康姆的论断极富洞见，即西奇威克的《伦理学方法》（1874）[6]的出版是伦理学史上的一个分水岭。

同之前的道德哲学家不同，西奇威克和他的支持者否认存在任何从类别本身来说就应该禁止的行为。所以，就彼得·辛格最喜欢的例子而言，杀死婴儿这一行为不受禁止——假设婴儿是残疾儿，而且其父母想杀死他。根据彼得·辛格的观点，这是因为婴儿并不具备理性自我意识或人格。故而他在专著《实践伦理学》中如此总结："不能杀人的理由并不适用于新生婴儿。"[7]安斯康姆的道德论点在这里尤为重要，因为当下的后果论者仅仅从成本效益分析的角度来考量杀婴这样凶残的行为。

安斯康姆在其文章中也批判了康德伦理学。《现代道德哲学》发表之后，康德伦理学开始受到更多人的关注。或许当今最著名的康德道德哲学家当属哈佛大学的克里斯汀·科尔斯戈德*，她于1996年发表的专著《规范性的来源》是对其哲学立场的系统性辩护。虽然安斯康姆认为个人为自我立法的观点是荒诞的，但科尔斯戈德认为自我反省有可能让人们成为自身的道德权威。[8]然而，由于"权威"通常意味着更大的权力对更小权力的支配状态，所以我们尚不清楚科尔斯戈德的叙述究竟是如何推翻了安斯康姆在《现代道德哲学》中的观点。

1. G. E. M. 安斯康姆:《人类生活、行为和伦理学》，玛丽·吉奇和卢克·高莫里编，埃克塞特：学术印记出版社，2005 年，Kindle 版。

2. 乔纳森·贝内特："道德与后果"，载《关于人类价值的坦纳讲座》第 2 卷，斯特林·麦克穆林编，盐湖城：犹他大学出版社，1981 年，第 110—111 页。

3. 乔纳森·贝内特:《行为本身》，纽约：牛津大学出版社，1995 年，第 194—225 页。

4. G. E. M. 安斯康姆："现代道德哲学"，《哲学》第 33 卷，1958 年第 124 期，第 1 页。

5. 卡塔日娜·德·拉扎里-博德克和彼得·辛格:《世界观：西奇威克和当代伦理学》，牛津：牛津大学出版社，2014 年。

6. 亨利·西奇威克:《伦理学方法》，第 7 版，印第安纳波利斯：哈克特出版社，1981 年。

7. 彼得·辛格:《实践伦理学》，剑桥：剑桥大学出版社，1979 年，第 124 页。

8. 克里斯汀·科尔斯戈德:《规范性的来源》，剑桥：剑桥大学出版社，1996 年，第 19—20 页。

12 未来展望

要点 🔑

- 《现代道德哲学》仍将是一篇重要的文本，因为它不仅强有力地批判了后果论和康德伦理学，还提出了替代理论。
- 此文使德性伦理学作为一种道德哲学思想而重新焕发生机。
- 关于德性伦理学的研究还将在各个方向蓬勃发展。

潜力

G. E. M. 安斯康姆的《现代道德哲学》改变了 20 世纪和 21 世纪的道德哲学，在未来还将是一篇具有影响力的文章。此文继续对后果论和康德伦理学进行清晰而严密的批判。此文仍将是哲学学生的必读著作，因为它对道德责任的本质提出了深刻的质疑，并对哲学史上最具影响力的几位道德思想家的理论进行了对比分析，它的发表是道德哲学中德性伦理学发展史上的分水岭。

此文在未来最大的潜力在于它能激发哲学家从事德性伦理学的研究。有迹象表明，尽管德性伦理学目前依然是一个比较小众的视角，但它将日益受到关注，在学术严谨性上也日臻完善。具体而言，德性伦理学已经开始被应用于众多领域，例如应用伦理学*（道德哲学的分支，专注于将道德原则应用于具体情形）及其分支生物伦理学*（研究医学和环境伦理问题），和政治哲学。例如，2013 年一部关于"应用德性伦理学"的文选得以出版，题为《行动中的德性：应用德性伦理学最新文选》[1]。文选涉及一系列主题，包括《值得尊重的商业管理者的德性》和《谦卑和环境德性伦理学》。

同样，《剑桥德性伦理学词典》[2] 也于 2013 年首次出版，此外，还有数十篇关于德性主题的文章和专著得以发表。

> "在一定程度上，在一定范围内，安斯康姆的文章改变了道德哲学，而且在很多人看来，这种改变是向好的改变。"
>
> —— 安东尼·奥希尔：《现代道德哲学》

未来方向

虽然《现代道德哲学》为道德哲学开辟了新的方向，但有很多方面尚需进一步发展——其中包括对道德心理学的哲学分析、对德性的阐释和对"最重要的，人的兴旺"[3]的理解。这些主题继续朝着引人入胜的方向发展。比如，美国哲学家玛莎·努斯鲍姆就是一位专注于探讨人类兴旺的当代德性伦理学家。她发表了多部关于道德心理学的重要作品，强调爱、同情、悲伤、羞愧和厌恶等情绪在伦理思考中的重要性。她和 1998 年诺贝尔经济学奖得主阿马蒂亚·森合作，建构福利经济学的"可行能力"理论，探讨兴旺生活所需的核心能力。

努斯鲍姆列举了多种必不可少的能力，其中包括形成情感依恋的能力、推理的能力、玩乐的能力和保持健康的能力。这种能力理论可用于比较和衡量国际发展，并有助于形成人类发展指数，这是一种衡量社会发展水平的国际指标。或许德性伦理学运动的这一方向——与政治学和经济学相关的人类兴旺和人类德性——将成为最富有成效的研究领域之一。

小结

《现代道德哲学》在 20 世纪的道德哲学领域依然是最重要的著作之一。在此文中，G. E. M. 安斯康姆将敏锐的分析视角投向后果论、康德伦理学和契约主义，并发现这三个流派要么不道德，要么在概念上缺乏内在一致性。

她发现后果论建立在"快乐"概念之上，而这一概念本身存疑，从而导致一些不道德的结论（例如，后果论者承认存在这样的可能性：判处无辜者死刑是"正确的"事情——假设这样做会带来一些积极的总体后果）。安斯康姆认为，这种观点是一些"思维堕落"之人的典型特征。[4]康德伦理学建立在为自我立法的概念之上，而她发现这一概念缺乏内在一致性。契约主义让道德判断取决于任一时间大多数人偶然的信念，而这样又会导致灾难性的道德结论。

此外，安斯康姆还对"责任""应该"和"正确"等"道德"术语的性质提出质疑，认为当代哲学家使用的这些概念毫无意义，因为他们不再相信神圣立法者的存在。这是因为，这些概念从本质上而言都是社会概念——你被一个更强大的力量命令做什么，或禁止做什么。然而，安斯康姆督促读者去寻找另一种方式来讨论人类行为的善恶。她认为，这一方法将依赖于"正义""德性"和"慈善"等内涵丰富的概念。安斯康姆的这一想法推动了德性伦理学运动的发展，德性伦理学在过去40年的道德哲学领域影响巨大。

上述成就使得《现代道德哲学》成为道德哲学史上最重要的作品之一。每一个读者都能够从安斯康姆在此文中提出的问题和论点中获益，此文为那些想要理解从20世纪中期至今的道德哲学发展状态的人提供了精彩的介绍。

---

1. 米歇尔·W.奥斯丁编：《行动中的德性：应用德性伦理学最新文选》，贝辛斯托克：帕尔格雷夫·麦克米伦，2013年。

2. 丹尼尔·C.拉塞尔编：《剑桥德性伦理学词典》，剑桥：剑桥大学出版社，2013年。

3. G. E. M.安斯康姆："现代道德哲学"，《哲学》第33卷，1958年第124期，第1—16页。

4. 安斯康姆："现代道德哲学"，第14页。

术语表

1. **行为理论**：哲学分支，研究人类行为的本质。其探讨的问题包括思维、决定论和自由意志。

2. **分析哲学**：一套哲学研究方法，注重概念和语言的详尽分析。这是英国和美国占主导地位的研究方法，其来源是 19 世纪晚期和 20 世纪初期剑桥大学的哲学研究。

3. **古代**：在哲学领域，古希腊罗马哲学的跨度大约是公元前 400 年至公元 200 年。代表性人物有柏拉图、亚里士多德和西塞罗。

4. **应用伦理学**：道德哲学分支，关注道德原理在具体情境中的应用。它还可以继续划分为"生物伦理学"和科技伦理学等分支。

5. **亚里士多德伦理观**：主要来自古希腊哲学家亚里士多德的伦理学理论。亚里士多德将伦理学建立在德性和 eudaimonia（意思相当于"幸福"）的概念之上。

6. **生物伦理学**：道德哲学分支，关注医学伦理学、环境伦理学、动物治疗伦理学。主要在 20 世纪 60 年代发展起来。

7. **原子弹轰炸广岛和长崎**：1945 年，美国在哈里·S.杜鲁门总统的授意下轰炸了日本主要城市广岛和长崎，以尽快结束第二次世界大战。这一行动备受争议，被很多人认为是对平民的大屠杀。

8. **绝对命令**：在任何情况下都适用的命令；指一个人必须永远根据其选择作为普世法则的原则办事的理论。

9. **后果论**：安斯康姆在《现代道德哲学》中发明的术语，现在使用非常广泛。它指任何仅仅通过行为后果来定义行为道德价值的道德哲学。

10. **契约主义**：一种道德理论，认为一个共同体成员之间存在隐性的契约，而这种契约构成了道德责任的基础。

11. **道义论**：一种强调义务的道德哲学。康德的伦理哲学是最典型的道义论例证；道义论认为每个有理性的人都有义务遵守绝对命令。

12. **决定论**：一种哲学观点，认为宇宙间的任何事情（包括所有的人类行为）都是由物理世界之前的状态通过因果关系所决定的。

13. **神圣律令伦理学 / 神圣律法伦理学**：一种道德哲学理论，宣称具有神令特征的行为是强制性行为。

14. **伦理反实在论**：认为道德事实并不存在的观点。因为后果论指唯有后果具备道德价值的观点，所以可以说，一个人如果是后果论者，那么他 / 她要么是伦理反实在论者，要么是伦理实在论者。

15. **伦理直觉主义**：一种伦理学观点，认为个体知道道德真实，是因为个体能够通过直觉能力直接获得道德事实。这一理论是由哲学家亨利·西奇威克和 G. E. 摩尔发展而来。

16. **伦理学**：哲学分支学科，关注道德的理论和实践问题。它首先试图回答"善的生活的本质是什么？"和"我们应该怎么生活？"等问题。

17. **康德伦理学**：一种道德责任理论（有时候又被称为"道义论"），认为一个人的责任是依据自己认为的普世道德原则来行事。

18. **伦理学的律法概念**：使用"责任""应该""正确"和"允许"等法律语言的伦理学概念。这种伦理学概念来自早期基督教对上帝颁布的神圣律法的信仰。

19. **医学伦理学**：应用伦理学分支，关注医学的伦理学。核心主题包括病人和医生的自主性、堕胎、安乐死、人体医学实验。

20. **中世纪**：哲学的中世纪时期大约是从公元 400 年到 1400 年。在西方，中世纪哲学的主要特征是基督教哲学思考和神学思考。

21. **形而上学**：对现实的终极本质的研究。

22. **道德责任**：指在哲学上对某人做什么或不做什么的要求。通常认为道德责任凌驾于其他的要求之上——不管是一己私利，还是社会期待。

23. **道德哲学**：伦理学的另一个名称。

24. **自然主义谬误**：哲学家 G. E. 摩尔提出的概念。摩尔认为，对一个物体的任何自然属性，我们都可以考察这一属性是好的还是坏的；因此把善本身与这一属性相等同是错误的。

25. **进步主义**：一种将"进步"视为最高政治目标的社会和政治观点。它与伦理学上的后果论关系密切。

26. **罗马天主教**：基督教的一种形式，可以追溯至耶稣基督最早信徒的生平。作为世界上最大的基督教教派，罗马天主教具有培养世界一流哲学家的传统。

27. **功利主义**：一种道德和政治哲学，认为最好的行为是带来最大数量人群的最大程度幸福的行为。这一思想最伟大的倡导者是社会和法律改革家杰里米·边沁和约翰·斯图亚特·穆勒。

28. **维多利亚时代**：维多利亚女王统治英国的时期：1837—1901 年。这一时期的特征是英国帝国主义和工业化。

29. **德性伦理学**：规范伦理学的一种立场，通过正义、睿智和慷慨等德性的获得和遵循来定义善的生活。

30. **德性**：通过人类行为表现出来的人格倾向。它们包括正义、节制和坚毅，它们构成了道德哲学中德性伦理学立场的核心。

31. **第二次世界大战**（1939—1945）：人类历史上最大的一次武装冲突。第二次世界大战中，同盟国（例如英国、美国、苏联和中国）与轴心国（纳粹德国、意大利和日本）作战。它导致了世界现代化进程中一段最快速的发展时期。

人名表

1. **罗伯特·亚当斯**（1937 年生），美国哲学家，研究道德哲学和形而上学。亚当斯最重要的贡献是关于道德责任的神圣律令理论的作品，即他的专著《有限的善和无限的善》（1999）。

2. **托马斯·阿奎那**（1225—1274）：中世纪一位极具影响力的神学家、哲学家和教育家。

3. **亚里士多德**（公元前 384—322）：古希腊哲学家，首次发明了"伦理"一词。他的伦理哲学的核心是通过达到极端行为之间的中庸状态来完善德性。

4. **乔纳森·贝内特**（1930 年生）：美国雪城大学哲学系的名誉教授。他专注于研究心灵哲学和哲学史。

5. **杰里米·边沁**（1748—1832）：英国哲学家和社会改革家，被认为是功利主义哲学流派的先驱。他认为一个行为的道德价值取决于它创造了多少快乐，阻止或减轻了多少痛苦。

6. **西蒙·布莱克本**（1944 年生）：英国著名的哲学家，剑桥大学已退休的伯特兰·罗素哲学教授。他在休谟哲学学派的著作包括《传播词语》（1984）和《准实在论论文集》。

7. **菲利帕·富特**（1920—2010）：英国哲学家，其作品主要将职业伦理哲学的讨论重点转向了德性和罪恶，而非后果或义务。

8. **威廉·弗兰克纳**（1908—1994）：颇具影响力的美国哲学家，曾执教于密歇根大学。他的研究领域是道德哲学，最具影响的作品是专著《伦理学》（1963）。

9. **彼得·吉奇**（1916—2013）：英国哲学家，研究逻辑和道德哲学。他最著名的作品是专著《德性》（1977）和文章《归因论》（1960）。

10. **R. M. 黑尔**（1919—2002）：20 世纪英国重要的道德哲学家。他是一个功利主义理论家，最重要的作品是《道德语言》（1952）。

11. **斯坦利·哈弗罗斯**（1940 年生）：基督教伦理学家，杜克大学神学院退休的吉尔伯特·T. 罗教授。他的主要作品有《人格与基督教人生》（1975）和《和平的国度》（1983）。

12. **大卫·休谟**（1711—1776）：极具影响力的苏格兰经验主义哲学家，著有《自然宗教对话录》（1779）和《道德原理研究》（1751）。他的道德理论试图将伦理学建立在人类情绪或感情之上。

13. **罗莎琳德·赫斯特豪斯**（1943 年生）：新西兰奥克兰大学哲学教授。她是著名的新亚里士多德德性伦理学家，她的主要作品有文章《德性理论与堕胎》（1991）和专著《德性伦理学》（1999）。

14. **伊曼努尔·康德**（1724—1804）：欧洲思想史上启蒙运动时期（约 1750—1900 年，主要特征是科学和哲学领域的剧烈变革，以及对理性力量的不断增长的信心）最有影响力的哲学家之一。他发表多部著作，其中包括《纯粹理性批判》（1781）和《道德形而上学原理》（1785），他认为伦理学应该建立在理性的基础之上。

15. **克里斯汀·科尔斯戈德**（1952 年生）：哈佛大学哲学教授，康德道德哲学家，最重要的作品是专著《规范性的来源》（1996）。

16. **阿拉斯戴尔·麦金太尔**（1929 年生）：苏格兰道德哲学家，曾在美国几所主要大学任教。他最重要的作品是关于德性伦理学的，包括《追寻美德》（1981）和《依赖性的理性动物：人类为什么需要德性》（1999）。

17. **约翰·斯图亚特·穆勒**（1806—1873）：英国哲学家和法律改革家，曾师从杰里米·边沁，并发展了边沁的功利主义思想。

18. **G. E. 摩尔**（1873—1958）：英国哲学家，曾因"自然主义谬误"的观点而闻名于剑桥，他试图证明"善"等价值判断术语并不能等同于快感等自然术语。

19. **凯·尼尔森**（1926 年生）：道德哲学家、加拿大卡尔加里大学名誉教授。他的作品包括《没有上帝的伦理学》（1971）。

20. **帕特里克·诺埃尔-史密斯**（1914—2006）：英国道德哲学家和功利

主义者。他最重要的作品是《伦理学》（1956）。

21. 玛莎·努斯鲍姆（1947 年生）：芝加哥大学法律和伦理学恩斯特·弗洛因德杰出贡献教授。发表著作《善的脆弱性》（1985）和《思想的剧变：情感的智慧》（2001），她致力于用亚里士多德的思想来补充康德伦理学。

22. 安东尼·奥希尔：英国哲学家，白金汉大学教授，皇家哲学学院院长。他发表的作品包括《追求进步》（1999）。

23. 柏拉图（约公元前 427—347 年）：历史上最重要的哲学家之一。苏格拉底的学生，他的对话录涵盖了整个哲学领域的大多数基本问题，例如伦理学、政治学、知识和上帝等。

24. 菲利普·L.奎恩（1940—2004）：哲学家和神学家，作为一名物理学和伦理学哲学学者而闻名。

25. 约翰·罗尔斯（1921—2002）：哈佛大学教授，20 世纪最有影响力的政治哲学家之一。他发表于 1971 年的代表作《正义论》为众多当代自由政治理论奠定了基础。

26. D.J.李克特：弗吉尼亚军事学院的道德哲学家，发表《安斯康姆之后的伦理学》（2000）和《安斯康姆的道德哲学》（2011）。

27. 阿马蒂亚·森（1933 年生）：印度经济学家，诺贝尔奖得主。他提出了福利经济的概念，该概念建立在德性伦理学影响下的可行能力理论之上。

28. 亨利·西奇威克（1838—1900）：英国功利主义哲学家和经济学家，他提倡妇女接受高等教育。如今他已经不大为人所知。

29. 彼得·辛格（1946 年生）：澳大利亚道德哲学家。他或许是当今世界最重要的功利主义者，他的作品包括《实用伦理学》（1979）和《动物解放：我们对待动物的新伦理学》（1975）。

30. 哈里·S.杜鲁门（1884—1972）：美国第 33 任总统，执政时间为 1945—1953 年。他在第二次世界大战中通过授权对日本广岛和长崎投放原子弹而迫使日本投降，此举导致数十万人死亡。

31. **路德维希·维特根斯坦**（1889—1951）：出生在奥地利、主要在英国工作的哲学家。他去世后发表的代表作《哲学研究》（1953）被他的得意门生伊丽莎白·安斯康姆校对并从德语翻译为英语，该著作在英国 20 世纪哲学史上具有极大的影响力。

WAYS IN TO THE TEXT

- G. E. M. Anscombe was a British philosopher best known for her writing on ethics*.

- Her paper "Modern Moral Philosophy" investigated notions such as moral obligation* in increasingly secular societies.

- Anscombe's text helped modernize moral philosophy and reevaluated ethics in contemporary philosophy.

Who Was G. E. M. Anscombe?

Elizabeth (G. E. M.) Anscombe, the author of the paper "Modern Moral Philosophy" (1958), was one of the most important and accomplished philosophers of the twentieth century. Her writing on ethics and moral philosophy was highly influential, and she pioneered contemporary action theory.*

Anscombe studied at Oxford University, obtaining a degree in Classics and Philosophy in 1941; later, she worked at Cambridge University, where she befriended the Austrian philosopher Ludwig Wittgenstein.* One of his most devoted students, she went on to translate his work. His influence on her was considerable: even after she returned to Oxford, she traveled back to Cambridge on a weekly basis to attend his lectures. Like Wittgenstein, Anscombe is known for her sharp analytic insights.

Anscombe is known for her strong Roman Catholic* beliefs, her conservative views on sexual ethics, and her long-held opposition to nuclear arms. Controversially, she opposed contraception and homosexual acts. Her views inspired the creation of a student organization promoting chastity and traditional sexual values—the

Anscombe Society, which established branches at Princeton, MIT, and several other universities. She staunchly opposed the use of atomic weapons at the end of World War II and, in 1956, she publicly criticized Oxford University's decision to award an honorary degree to US president Harry S. Truman,* citing his approval of the nuclear bombing of the Japanese cities of Hiroshima and Nagasaki.* This action was indefensible, Anscombe believed, because, even if it had brought an immediate end to the war and reduced the total number of lives lost, it was aimed at killing innocent civilians.

What Does "Modern Moral Philosophy" Say?

Anscombe's most important work is her paper "Modern Moral Philosophy." From the outset, she identifies that the paper contains "three theses":[1] that concepts of moral obligation were irrelevant in a secular society; that there were virtually no differences between the major British moral philosophers (that is, the consequentialists,* who judged the moral value of an action from its consequences); and that without an "adequate philosophy of psychology,"[2] moral philosophy becomes a fruitless field of study.

In her first point, Anscombe proposes that some ideas are the remnants of a Christian tradition that alone can issue moral laws. These include moral obligation and duty and the distinction between actions that are morally right and those that are morally wrong. A firm believer in God, Anscombe does not dispute divine power but, rather, argues that a secular society can no longer use the language of ethics. The word "ought," for instance, or related notions such as moral obligation (things we are obliged to do on the grounds of morality), could not be used because secular societies, by their very nature, were detached from God.

"Ought" denotes the command of a moral authority, which, in the past, would have been God. In a secular society, though, God is no longer the sole voice of authority able to command us to behave in certain ways. Without this connection to God, she argues, such words and concepts have lost their meaning.

Anscombe's second proposition is that it is impossible to distinguish between the English moral philosophers of the previous 75 years. There was no genuine debate going on in moral philosophy, she claims, and all its proponents had uniformly rejected God and fundamentally agreed on consequentialism—the view that any action is only morally relevant in terms of its foreseeable consequences, and any rules of behavior can in some circumstances be broken. Though supposedly different from one another, all contemporary moral philosophies lead, she argued, to this kind of position—a view that, ultimately, could be used to defend the execution of an innocent person.

If someone with a gun told you that she would kill 20 innocent people unless you killed one innocent person (and you had good reason to believe her), according to the consequentialist position it would be right for you to kill the innocent person and wrong for you to fail to kill the innocent person since the consequences of killing the innocent person are preferable to those of not killing her.[3] This was completely at odds with the Christian morality that had dominated Europe for more than 1,000 years, according to which certain actions were immoral, regardless of their consequences.

Finally, she suggests that moral philosophy needs an alternative model, based on psychology. She argues that there can be no interpretation of moral right and wrong that excludes God, and ethics can no longer be based on divine rules. Instead, Anscombe suggests returning to secular concepts of practical reasoning, virtue, and justice derived from the work of the ancient Greek philosopher Aristotle.* So, instead of an action being morally wrong, it would be unjust. Virtue ethics*—an approach to ethics that identifies the good life in terms of attaining, and acting in accord with, virtues such as justice, wisdom and generosity—could exist in a non-moral sense and without the need for divine authority.

Why Does "Modern Moral Philosophy" Matter?

Anscombe made highly acclaimed contributions to many topics, including action theory (a subfield of philosophy that analyzes the nature of human action), metaphysics* (the study of the ultimate nature of reality), and the work of Wittgenstein. Her essay "Modern Moral Philosophy" matters, in particular, because of its lasting impact on ethics. It helped revive the school of moral philosophy called virtue ethics and many later philosophers took up the conceptual and moral problems it raised. A few of the most important include the English philosopher Philippa Foot* in *Virtues and Vices and Other Essays*,[4] the influential Scottish philosopher Alasdair MacIntyre* in *AfterVirtue*,[5] and the prominent virtue ethicist Rosalind Hursthouse* of the University of Auckland in *On Virtue Ethics*.[6]

More fundamentally, Anscombe's text tackles such questions as the importance of acting ethically and the value of ethics to philosophy. She suggests that there is not much point in doing moral philosophy unless important concepts such as obligation, justice, and virtue are completely understood. The text demands a new, clearer thinking and calls for philosophers to explain their terms and concepts properly.

Anscombe's essay helped reform moral philosophy. In it, she attacked consequentialism and ethics derived from the work of the influential German philosopher Immanuel Kant,* describing them as immoral or simply incoherent. She challenged the consequentialist position that condemning the innocent to death could be the "right" thing to do if it could have some positive effect overall. She described this idea as corrupt, believing that a wider, universal human morality could not depend on fluctuating majority decisions.

In a contemporary world accustomed to mounting civilian deaths in international conflicts carried out in the name of the greater good, Anscombe's account of morality offers a radical alternative. This alternative places weight on the justice or wisdom or temperance of actions themselves, rather than on their consequences.

---

1. G. E. M. Anscombe, "Modern Moral Philosophy," *Philosophy* 33, no. 124 (1958): 1.

2. Anscombe, "Modern Moral Philosophy," 1.

3. This example is from Bernard Williams and J. J. C. Smart, *Utilitarianism: For and Against* (Cambridge: Cambridge University Press, 1973), 97–116.

4. Philippa Foot, *Virtues and Vices and Other Essays in Moral Philosophy* (Berkeley and Los Angeles: University of California Press, 1978).

5. See Alasdair MacIntyre, *After Virtue*, 3rd revised edition (London: Duckworth, 2007).

6. See Rosalind Hursthouse, *On Virtue Ethics* (Oxford: Oxford University Press, 2001).

SECTION 1
INFLUENCES

THE AUTHOR AND THE HISTORICAL CONTEXT

KEY POINTS

- "Modern Moral Philosophy" transformed moral philosophy.* It criticized the consequentialist* position that an action's morality should be judged on its consequences and the ethical philosophy derived from the German thinker Immanuel Kant* for relying on a defunct concept of moral obligation* (a requirement upon an individual to do something or refrain from doing something). In their place, it offered an alternative moral theory, now known as virtue ethics,* which emphasizes acting in accordance with such virtues as justice, prudence, and temperance (moderation).

- Elizabeth (G. E. M.) Anscombe was a practicing Roman Catholic* who worked at Oxford and Cambridge universities during a high point in analytic philosophy* (a set of philosophical methods that focus on the analysis of language and concepts). She was a favorite student of the influential Austrian thinker Ludwig Wittgenstein* and collated, edited, and translated his work.

- Writing in the aftermath of World War II,* injustices perpetrated by the Allies—the forces led by Britain and the United States— especially the atomic bombs dropped by the United States on two Japanese cities, provoked Anscombe to criticize the consequentialist morality then prevalent.

Why Read This Text?

G. E. M. Anscombe's paper "Modern Moral Philosophy"[1] was published in the journal *Philosophy* in 1958. In it, Anscombe challenges the very foundations of moral philosophy (inquiry into ethics)* as it was practiced at the time. She argues that there is no point in moral philosophy until the important concepts—obligation, justice, and virtue—are sufficiently analyzed and understood, and points a finger at contemporary moral philosophers who, she says, use these notions without any clear meaning. She highlights the concept of "moral obligation" or "moral ought," claiming that they came from a conception of ethics derived from divine law—but this had long been abandoned by philosophers as a historical product of Christianity.

In other words, as Christianity was gradually abandoned in philosophical circles, the concept of moral obligation became increasingly meaningless. Philosophers were using words that, essentially, had lost their meaning.

Anscombe also invented the term "consequentialist" to describe the philosophical view that a moral judgment can only ever be made about an action by examining its expected consequences. She raises serious objections both to this idea and to Kantian ethics,* which held, in short, that an action is moral if and only if you could make it into a universal law. So, for Kant, telling falsehoods was wrong because it is impossible rationally to will that everyone everywhere should always tell falsehoods.

Finally, Anscombe's essay is also very important because it launched the ideas that would become the discipline of virtue ethics.

⌐ *"It is not possible for us at present to do moral philosophy."*
——G. E. M. Anscombe, "Modern Moral Philosophy" ⌟

Author's Life

Gertrude Elizabeth Margaret Anscombe was the daughter of a schoolmaster and a Classics scholar. She was educated at Sydenham College and as a teenager read a great deal of philosophy and theology, becoming a convinced Roman Catholic* as a result. Anscombe studied at Oxford University, where she obtained a degree in Classics and Philosophy in 1941. After undergraduate studies, she pursued a career as an academic philosopher at both Oxford and Cambridge. She would go on to hold the chair in philosophy at the University of Cambridge from 1970 to 1986, and her most important philosophical works are "Modern Moral Philosophy" (1958), *Intention* (1957), and *Causality and Determination* (1971).[2]

Anscombe wrote "Modern Moral Philosophy" in 1958 while a research fellow at Somerville College, Oxford. She had been a student and close friend of the highly influential Austrian thinker Ludwig Wittgenstein,* and became an executor of his work after his death in 1951; Wittgenstein's influence can be seen throughout Anscombe's other major works, including "Modern Moral Philosophy." She was married to another Catholic philosopher, Peter T. Geach,* with whom she had seven children. In addition to her philosophical papers, of which "Modern Moral Philosophy" is among the most important, Anscombe wrote several papers specifically for a Roman Catholic readership.

Anscombe was a famously independent philosopher. She gained some notoriety when, in 1956, she publicly objected to the honorary degree that Oxford University awarded to US President

Harry S. Truman.* Her grounds were that he had been responsible for the nuclear bombing and mass killing of the people of the Japanese cities of Hiroshima and Nagasaki* during World War II. It had been argued by some that Truman's action was acceptable because, though the bombs killed hundreds of thousands of Japanese citizens, it probably prevented even more deaths of US and Japanese soldiers. Anscombe did not consider this a legitimate action, however, because even if it brought the war to an immediate end, its aim was to kill innocent civilians.

Author's Background

Perhaps the most relevant social factor behind Anscombe's essay is the social progressivism* of the post-World War II period of British history. Progressivism tended to remove long-standing moral prohibitions such as the rule against bombing civilians as a means of shortening the war. The justification for this was that, by lifting such restrictions, the world's total suffering would be minimized and its total pleasure maximized. Anscombe cited these attitudes in her radio address "Does Oxford Moral Philosophy Corrupt the Youth?",[3] convinced that some actions are categorically wrong in their own right.

This makes Anscombe a moral absolutist. She argues that Oxford moral philosophy is not responsible for corrupting youth— it is merely a reflection of the social current of progressivism: "This philosophy is conceived perfectly in the spirit of the time and might be called the philosophy of the flattery of that spirit."[4] Anscombe's condemnation of progressivism rests on what she sees as the purpose of moral philosophy: to teach students to question popular ethical trends. This, she said, was something her colleagues utterly failed to do.

---

1. G. E. M. Anscombe, "Modern Moral Philosophy," *Philosophy* 33, no. 124 (1958): 1–19.

2. See G. E. M. Anscombe, "Modern Moral Philosophy"; Anscombe, *Intention* (Oxford: Blackwell, 1957); and Anscombe, *Causality and Determination: An Inaugural Lecture* (Cambridge: Cambridge University Press, 1971).

3. G. E. M. Anscombe, "Does Oxford Moral Philosophy Corrupt the Youth?", in *Human Life, Action and Ethics*, St. Andrews Studies in Philosophy and Public Policy, ed. Mary Geach and Luke Gormally (Exeter: Imprint Academic, 2005), Kindle edition; originally printed in *The Listener* 57 (February 14, 1957): 266–7, 271. The question posed to Anscombe in the title is a reference to ancient Athenian philosopher Socrates, who was executed on the charge of "corrupting the youth" when, in fact, he was merely training them to question the prevailing cultural assumptions of the time.

4. Anscombe, "Does Oxford Moral Philosophy Corrupt the Youth?", Kindle edition.

MODULE 2
ACADEMIC CONTEXT

KEY POINTS

- Moral philosophy is concerned with understanding what it is to be moral and how such terms as "right" and "wrong" should be used.
- Moral philosophy has four broad approaches: consequentialism,* which focuses solely on the consequences of an action; Kantian ethics,* which focuses on an individual deciding on his or her own moral rules; divine command ethics,* which focuses on obedience to God's law; and virtue ethics,* which focuses on understanding and developing the virtues.*
- Anscombe regarded consequentialism as deeply morally problematic. She proposed instead a return to the Aristotelian approach to ethics* bolstered by psychology.

The Work in Its Context

In "Modern Moral Philosophy," G. E. M. Anscombe surveys and critiques the main moral philosophies of the 1950s.

Moral philosophy deals with such themes as the nature of moral obligation* (a requirement upon an individual to do something or refrain from doing something), right action, and the good life. What is the purpose of life? "Consequentialism" (a term Anscombe invented) is the view that, morally speaking, only consequences matter. In other words, rules or prohibitions or divine commands are irrelevant, unless they contribute to good consequences. But in that case, it is the consequence—and not the rule or command—that makes the action morally good. A subdivision of consequentialism is utilitarianism,* which argues that only the production of pleasure and reduction of pain make an action moral.

The leading contemporary alternative to consequentialism was Kantian ethics, an approach that originated from the thought of the eighteenth-century German philosopher Immanuel Kant.* Kant highlights duties: norms or rules chosen for their own sake and not for their consequences; for him, duty underlies the morality of any action.

Divine command ethics is a form of morality that assumes the existence of a divinity who makes the rules we must obey; this is the approach of Christian morality.

Finally, virtue ethics was the preferred moral view in the classical world. Ancient Greek and Roman philosophers believed that the aim of ethics was the development and practice of the virtues (dispositions of character that are expressed in human action—such as temperance, wisdom, and courage).

> *"'Modern Moral Philosophy' also touched a nerve with philosophers who advocated one or the other of the condemned views. One reason for this was the rather dismissive or moralistic tone she took in some of her criticisms."*
>
> ——Julia Driver, "Gertrude Elizabeth Margaret Anscombe," in *Stanford Encyclopedia of Philosophy*

Overview of the Field

Consequentialism (usually known as utilitarianism) was an idea famously developed by the English philosopher and social reformer Jeremy Bentham.* In his 1789 book *An Introduction to the Principles of Morals and Legislation*[1] he famously argued that pleasure and pain are the two competing masters of humanity— they "govern us in all we do, in all we say, in all we think."[2] Bentham also suggested a calculus to determine the morality of an action according to how much pleasure it would produce and how much pain it would prevent or alleviate. Bentham's student, the philosopher John Stuart Mill, further developed this theory* in his influential 1861 book *Utilitarianism*.

According to Immanuel Kant, the originator of Kantian ethics, the individual "legislates" moral norms for him- or herself, based on what any rational person would do in a given situation. This is known as the "categorical imperative." As an example, Kant (and later "Kantians") have believed that a rational person would choose never to lie. This is because, if I were to lie in order to, say, swindle you out of money, then I would be implicitly endorsing others lying to me when it was to their financial advantage. We would lose the capacity to distinguish between truth and falsehood, and live in a contradictory, muddled fashion—something no rational thinker would choose.

The Greek philosopher Aristotle* is the most important figure in virtue ethics. The author of the influential *Nicomachean Ethics*, Aristotle saw the good life as being characterized by a particular kind of happiness called *eudaimonia* (Greek for "blessedness"). *Eudaimonia* is the ultimate good for human beings, and it is achieved by perfecting such virtues as courage, wisdom, temperance, and so on. Aristotle's virtue ethics, however, should not be thought of as focusing on "being good" as a mental state. On the contrary, "doing right actions" is the key to Aristotle's belief in "virtuous activity."[3]

Academic Influences

Anscombe was undoubtedly inspired by the twentieth-century philosopher Ludwig Wittgenstein,* who was at that time enormously influential on the philosophical thinking at Oxford and Cambridge universities. Anscombe was one of his graduate students, and she translated his *Philosophical Investigations* into English.[4] Wittgenstein influenced Anscombe's criticism of concepts like "ought" and "obligation." He had famously argued that "the meaning of a word is its use in the language."[5] Anscombe continually questions the meaning of such moral words as "obligation" and "ought" in common usage as these are words that referred to the rules of a divine lawgiver (God).

While Wittgenstein influenced Anscombe in the area of philosophical methodology and analysis of language, it is Aristotle who is probably Anscombe's most important influence in the field of moral philosophy. In the text, Anscombe contrasts all forms of modern moral philosophy with Aristotle's and proposes giving moral philosophy back its coherence by reviving the notion of the virtues, arguing: "Eventually it might be possible to advance to considering the concept of a virtue; with which, I suppose, we should be beginning some sort of study of ethics."[6]

In short, such rich concepts as "justice" or "prudence" could do the philosophical work that the words "ought" and "morally wrong" were employed to do in modern philosophy.

1. Jeremy Bentham, *An Introduction to the Principles of Morals and Legislation* (Oxford: Clarendon Press, 1907).

2. Jeremy Bentham, *Principles of Morals and Legislation*, 1; quoted in Julia Driver, "The History of Utilitarianism," *Stanford Encyclopedia of Philosophy* (Winter 2014 edition), ed. Edward N. Zalta, accessed October 6, 2015, http://plato.stanford.edu/entries/utilitarianism-history/.

3. Aristotle, *Nicomachean Ethics,* ed. and trans. Roger Crisp (Cambridge: Cambridge University Press, 2014), ix, 12.

4. Ludwig Wittgenstein, *Philosophical Investigations (Philosophische Untersuchungen) English & German*, trans. G. E. M. Anscombe (Oxford: Basil Blackwell, 1953).

5. Ludwig Wittgenstein, *Philosophical Investigations*, 4th edition, 2009, ed. and trans. P. M. S. Hacker and Joachim Schulte (Oxford: Wiley-Blackwell, 2009), 43.

6. G. E. M. Anscombe, "Modern Moral Philosophy," *Philosophy* 33, no. 124 (1958): 12–13.

MODULE 3
THE PROBLEM

KEY POINTS

* The key question in G. E. M. Anscombe's "Modern Moral Philosophy" is: What is the nature and meaning of moral obligation?*

* For consequentialism,* we are morally obliged to do whatever results in the best consequences; ethical anti-realism* contends that there are no moral facts or obligations.

* Anscombe proposed abandoning consequentialism because the idea of "moral obligation" was a hangover from the concept of divine laws, a concept in which people no longer generally believed.

Core Question

G. E. M. Anscombe's central inquiry in "Modern Moral Philosophy" is into the nature and meaning of moral obligation. She raised the question in a provocative and unique way, arguing that moral obligation and the moral "ought" had no meaning in the philosophical discourse of her day. Anscombe strongly opposed the consequentialist justifications of what she considered morally outrageous acts such as the atomic bombing of the Japanese cities of Hiroshima and Nagasaki* by US President Harry S. Truman* at the end of World War II; the killing of hundreds of thousands of innocent civilians could be justified by consequentialist thought so long as it saved more lives in the long run. Anscombe believed such thinking was utterly out of step with traditional morality.

Consequentialists had answered the question of moral obligation by reducing it solely to a matter of consequences. Anscombe, however, observed that this sense of moral obligation has no direct parallel in either the language or the moral philosophy of the Greek philosopher Aristotle.* She suggested that the concept of moral obligation is a residue of a Christian belief in divine legislative authority: because of God's supreme power, authority, and wisdom, we must behave morally. But, argues Anscombe, consequentialists do not believe in God, or, if they do, they do not believe that divine authority creates our moral obligations. As a result, they use the concept of "moral obligation" without explaining its meaning. Anscombe proposes that moral philosophers jettison "obligation" and "ought" as leftovers from Christian morality and instead use richer virtue concepts like justice and temperance.

> "My mother settled down to read the standard modern ethicists and was appalled. The thing these people had in common, which had made Truman drop the bomb and dons defend him, was a belief which Anscombe called 'consequentialism'."
> —— Mary Geach, Introduction to *Human Life, Action and Ethics: Essays by G. E. M. Anscombe*

The Participants

Anscombe's essay focuses on the state of moral philosophy in the first half of the twentieth century. Two of Anscombe's British predecessors are key to understanding the context in which she was writing.

The first of these, Henry Sidgwick,* was the foremost British philosopher of the Victorian period (1837–1901).* His most influential work in moral philosophy was *Methods of Ethics* (1874), a culmination of the utilitarian* ethical tradition (the approach to moral philosophy according to which the best action is the one that produces the greatest happiness in the greatest number). According to historians, Sidgwick "set the agenda for most of the twentieth-century debates between utilitarians and their critics."[1] He was a unique thinker in his time and tried to combine utilitarianism with Immanuel Kant's* deontology* (an ethical philosophy founded on the notion of duty) to form a theory he called ethical "intuitionism."* Sidgwick argues that, while we have certain intuitions about our duty in a particular situation, those intuitions about morality eventually collapse into utilitarian principles. So an individual may intuitively perceive the duty not to strike an innocent stranger in the street, but the ultimate principle that makes such an action wrong is a utilitarian principle of preventing suffering. By implication, the principle that one should not strike a stranger can be overturned in the light of the good consequences it may bring about in the end.

The second important predecessor, British philosopher G. E. Moore,* continued Sidgwick's combination of intuitionism and utilitarianism. A highly influential thinker, Moore was a fellow of Trinity College, Cambridge, and author of the voluminous *Principia Ethica* (1903). In *Principia*, he argued that "good" was not a natural property—that to identify "good" with any natural thing was to commit the "naturalistic fallacy."* In other words, it is always an open question whether any particular natural thing or natural fact is good. Moore concludes that the property "good" cannot exist independently of natural objects or states of affairs. In other words, the property of goodness is like the property of red: though redness is perceived in certain objects because of their physical characteristics, redness is distinct from those physical properties.

These two philosophers helped lay the groundwork for moral philosophy in Anscombe's day in two ways. First, they held to consequentialism in some form. Second, they created a gap between the natural facts of the world and the concepts "ought" and "right" and "obligation." For them, no everyday fact—like "the child is thirsty"—entails any particular moral injunction such as "I should give the child water."

The Contemporary Debate

In preparation for teaching a moral philosophy class at Oxford University in 1958, Anscombe made a survey of the modern moral philosophers. She seems to have started with the eighteenth-century Scottish philosopher David Hume* and Immanuel Kant, and continued with Sidgwick, Moore, and her own contemporaries. All of these philosophers shared a tendency to divide completely the "moral" sphere from the "natural" sphere. Hume had argued that there is no logical link between "is" statements and "ought" statements. So, for instance, the factual statement "God commands you to honor your parents" does not lead to the moral statement "You ought to honor your parents" because there is an unstated premise in between: "You ought to do whatever God commands."

This unstated premise already has an "ought" and so is a moral, rather than a factual, statement. Hume is pointing out a gap between the normal world of facts and the special world of "moral oughts."[2]

In this context, Anscombe cast a skeptical eye over all these thinkers, and applied to their moral philosophies the linguistic analysis she had learned from Ludwig Wittgenstein.* She concluded that, if words like "ought" and "obligation" gain their meaning by their relation to God, then they lost that meaning when they were used without it.

---

1. Barton Schultz, "Henry Sidgwick," *The Stanford Encyclopedia of Philosophy* (Summer 2015 edition), ed. Edward N. Zalta, accessed October 7, 2015, http://plato.stanford.edu/archives/sum2015/entries/sidgwick/.

2. David Hume, *Treatise of Human Nature*, ed. L. A. Selby-Bigge and P. H. Nidditch, 2nd edition (Oxford: Oxford University Press, 1978), 469–70.

MODULE 4
THE AUTHOR'S CONTRIBUTION

KEY POINTS

* Anscombe argued that moral obligation* is a leftover from a system of morality based on divine authority in which people no longer believed—therefore the concept should be dropped.

* This paved the way for virtue ethics,* an alternative to consequentialism* that focused on the virtues: justice and temperance, for example.

* Anscombe was influenced by the philosopher Wittgenstein's* linguistic analysis and applied it to the concept of moral obligation.

Author's Aims

The original groundbreaking idea in G. E. M. Anscombe's "Modern Moral Philosophy" is that the current "moral" sense of such terms as "ought," "obligation," "right and wrong," and "duty" is incoherent and arguably unnecessary. This sense of "moral" did not exist at all in the work of the Greek philosopher Aristotle,* who focused instead on the nature of the virtues—such as courage, justice, wisdom, and temperance—and their role in a flourishing human life. The absence of moral obligation in Aristotle's writings shows that a coherent theory of ethics does not need such a concept.

The notion of moral obligation is also, Anscombe argues, incoherent. She puts forward the hypothesis that the concept arose as a by-product of the 2,000 years or so of Christianity that came between Aristotle and the twentieth century. Its meaning depends, she says, on a belief in a divine legislator (God) because a superior power and authority is needed both to create a "law" and to enforce "obligations." So, for instance, the "law of the land" works because it is enacted by an entire nation, lending it the means to punish me for disobedience. Anscombe seems to suggest that there is a similar connection between God and moral obligation. This presented moral philosophers with a choice: either return to a religious conception of ethics or abandon talk of "ought" or "obligation" in favor of richer concepts like "justice," "virtues,""vice," and so on. This was unprecedented.

> *"First... it is not profitable at present for us to do moral philosophy... Second... the concepts of obligation, and duty—* ***moral*** *obligation and* ***moral*** *duty, that is to say... ought to be jettisoned if this is psychologically possible... Third... the differences between the well-known English writers on moral philosophy from Sidgwick to the present day are of little importance."*
> —— G. E. M. Anscombe, "Modern Moral Philosophy"

Approach

Anscombe's main aims in "Modern Moral Philosophy" are philosophical and public. Philosophically, the paper takes both an analytic approach, with its emphasis on language and definitions, and a historical approach. While Anscombe is interested in challenging the meaning of words like "ought," she is also interested in clarifying moral concepts. She uses Aristotle's moral philosophy as a foil against modern authors, writing: "Anyone who has read Aristotle's *Ethics* and has also read modern moral philosophy must be struck by the great contrasts between them."[1] While a historical approach to moral philosophy was not new, Anscombe's innovation was to apply Aristotle's thought to modern moral questions.

Anscombe had wider concerns, too, particularly what she viewed as a general moral decline in civic society. It stemmed, she believed, from consequentialism, which gave license to any kind of action, however seemingly immoral, on the grounds of its foreseeable consequences. In "Mr. Truman's Degree" (1958),[2] Anscombe argued that US president Harry S. Truman* had committed mass murder by authorizing the use of the atom bomb on the Japanese cities of Hiroshima and Nagasaki. Similarly, in "Does Oxford Philosophy Corrupt the Youth? " (1957), she claims that consequentialism has resulted in a mentality conducive to oppression: "Preventative measures means they want to go into people's homes and push them around not because they have 'done anything,' but just in case they do."[3]

Her worries about consequentialism clearly reach far beyond philosophy and into the problematic arena of public morality.

Contribution in Context

Anscombe was undoubtedly influenced by the philosopher Ludwig Wittgenstein and is sometimes referred to as his disciple.[4] She worked with the ordinary-language method that was popular at the time and can in part be traced to Wittgenstein, who seems to have believed that the way we use language ultimately gives words their meanings.

Anscombe uses this idea in the following way.

First, the concepts of "obligation" and "moral ought" were essentially borrowed from Jewish and Christian theology and adapted to Western philosophy under Christianity. The words gained their meaning, implies Anscombe, through their use in relation to God. However, after people have dismissed the concept of God, it is unclear in what sense "moral obligation" is used. We see this in Anscombe's treatment of the philosopher Immanuel Kant's* "categorical imperative";* for Kant, we are obligated to do the right thing because we can legislate for ourselves. According to Anscombe, however, Kant is simply borrowing a word that has only had meaning because of its use in relation to God; Kant's use empties it of all meaning.

---

1. G. E. M. Anscombe, "Modern Moral Philosophy," *Philosophy* 33, no. 124 (1958): 1.

2. G. E. M. Anscombe, "Mr. Truman's Degree," in *Ethics, Religion and Politics* (Oxford: Basil Blackwell, 1981).

3. G. E. M. Anscombe, "Does Oxford Moral Philosophy Corrupt the Youth?", in *Human Life, Action and Ethics*, St. Andrews Studies in Philosophy and Public Policy, ed. Mary Geach and Luke Gormally (Exeter: Imprint Academic, 2005), Kindle edition.

4. Peter J. Conradi, *Iris Murdoch: A Life* (London: HarperCollins, 2002), 266: "Since [Iris Murdoch] was too late to hear Wittgenstein lecture, his influence reached her mainly through disciples such as Elizabeth Anscombe."

SECTION 2
IDEAS

MAIN IDEAS

KEY POINTS

- Anscombe's key themes are consequentialism,* ethical philosophy derived from the thought of the philosopher Immanuel Kant* (Kantian ethics),* moral obligation,* a law conception of ethics,* the Aristotelian approach to ethics,* and the virtues.*

- All modern moral philosophy, she argues, uses a concept of moral obligation that makes no sense without a belief in a God who makes moral laws.

- Anscombe argued that all modern moral philosophy was essentially the same—consequentialist. Consequentialism, she says, is not only conceptually confused, but also morally dangerous because it justifies immoral acts.

Key Themes

There are four primary themes in G. E. M. Anscombe's "Modern Moral Philosophy."

- The intelligibility question: in what sense can moral philosophers' current uses of "morally ought," "right," "wrong" and "obligation" be understood without belief in God?

- A plausible moral theory must be coherent and must not be immoral.

- Consequentialism, Kantianism, and contractualism* all fall short of these first two criteria in some way.

- There is a great divide between the ancient Greek philosopher Aristotle's* virtue ethics* and all ethical theories of moral philosophy formulated since the 1700s.

Together, these themes create a single, very deep, and multifaceted question: what is the meaning of moral terms like "ought," "right," and "obligation" for modern philosophers who reject belief in God? Among the possible answers she considers are that a) the will of society provides the grounding for "obligation," b) that self-legislation ("laws" made and observed by the self) provides it, or c) that consequences provide it.

Each of these answers, Anscombe argues, is either incoherent as a ground for the meaning of the word "ought" or is morally unacceptable. In contrast, she examines the virtue ethics of Aristotle, an approach founded on the observance of rich— or "thick"—values and concepts such as "wisdom," "courage," "justice," "truthfulness," "temperance" that require neither the "ought" and "obligation" concepts nor a divine legislator. Moral philosophers, Anscombe continues, are faced with a dilemma: either return to some form of belief in a divine legislator and keep notions of "ought" or pursue some version of Aristotle's virtue ethics.

> "Anscombe's... theses are the following: (1) the **profitability claim**: it is not at present profitable for us to do moral philosophy; (2) the **conceptual claim**: the concepts of 'moral obligation', 'moral duty,' what is 'morally right and wrong,' and 'ought' in its moral sense should be discarded; (3) the **triviality claim**: the differences between English moral philosophers since Sidgwick are of little significance."
>
> ——Roger Crisp, "Does Moral Philosophy Rest on a Mistake?"

Exploring the Ideas

First,it should be said that Anscombe does not argue that nonbelievers cannot use concepts like "moral obligation" and "ought." Instead, she says that, because these concepts originally gained their meaning by reference to God's law or God's commands, it is up to those who deny God's existence to explain the words' meaning and use.

Anscombe goes on to explore the most promising possible explanations of the concept of moral obligation—Kantianism, contractualism, and consequentialism—and she finds each, in turn, lacking.

The basic idea of Kantian ethics—the idea of legislating for oneself—is, she believes, incoherent. Kant had emphasized the individual's autonomy (self-rule) as his or her guiding ethical principle. But lawmaking, says Anscombe, requires a greater power or authority to govern a lesser power: "The concept of legislation requires superior power in the legislator."[1] So, in the political realm, a body such as a parliament or congress legislates, and the laws it passes are imposed on individuals who should then obey them. But since an individual cannot be both the legislator and the one legislated to, the analogy with political lawmaking does not hold.

Anscombe dismisses contractualism for moral, rather than strictly conceptual, reasons. Contractualism refers to any theory of morality that posits an implicit contract between members of a community that is supposed to ground moral obligation. If we must obey whichever moral norms the majority happens to choose, she argues, we will inevitably be subject to grossly unjust obligations. For example, if the majority were to choose tomorrow that races must be "kept pure" by preventing interracial marriage, it is difficult to see how contractualists could avoid making that a binding moral obligation.

Finally, Anscombe sees several flaws in consequentialism (any moral philosophy that defines the moral value of an action solely in terms of its consequences). Classical consequentialists assumed, she says, that they had a definite concept of pleasure; it was never established, however, whether pleasure was an internal impression or whether it was intrinsically tied up with the cause of that impression. Our language shows this, since we classify as pleasure both *feelings* ("There's a pleasant feeling in my arm") and *activities* ("Throwing a baseball is one of my pleasures."). Even if pleasure is an internal impression that all pleasant activities have in common, she continues, then choosing actions based on their pleasing consequences alone leads to disastrous moral results.

To illustrate this point Anscombe argues that judicious punishment of the innocent offers a model of injustice. But consequentialism cannot decide beforehand the morality of an unjust act like punishing the innocent: if a judge knows that condemning one innocent person to death will—for some reason—end up saving several other innocent lives, then that consequence means that the judge is morally obligated to condemn the innocent to death.

She argues that both divine law ethics* and Aristotelian ethics* determine that it is wrong to be unjust, whereas consequentialists will always allow circumstances in which it is right to commit such an unjust act.

Language and Expression

Anscombe was one of the greatest analytic philosophers* of the twentieth century, following a philosophical method that focuses on detailed conceptual and linguistic analysis.[2] So a good student of the text will pay attention both to her careful analysis and to her moral insight. Anscombe uses words in ways that can seem idiosyncratic to contemporary readers or nonphilosophers. For instance, "modern" describes philosophers roughly from the 1600s to her day—a broader range than is usually covered by "modern."

Anscombe coined the term "consequentialism"* in "Modern Moral Philosophy"; it has subsequently become the most common term for moral theories that base the rightness of an act upon consequences alone. She also reintroduced the philosophical use of the term "virtue"; virtue ethics or Aristotelianism is now considered an alternative to Kantianism and consequentialism.

While Anscombe's essay is aimed at a philosophical audience rather than a popular one, her paper "Does Oxford Moral Philosophy Corrupt the Youth?", which displays certain parallels to "Modern Moral Philosophy," works on a more popular level. Anscombe's writing is notoriously dense. Her daughter once remarked: "Her style is dense and unrepetitive, and it is hard to know sometimes whether it would be more clarificatory to go on to the next sentence, or to return to the previous one."[3] However, Anscombe is a very systematic thinker and defines words and concepts as she goes, and while she uses specialist language or examples, it is not in order to cloud her meaning but rather to illuminate it.

---

1. G. E. M. Anscombe, "Modern Moral Philosophy," *Philosophy* 33, no. 124 (1958): 2.

2. Peter J. Conradi, *Iris Murdoch: A Life* (London: HarperCollins, 2002), 283: "The most brilliant of her generation of British philosophers, Elizabeth Anscombe was from 1946 a Research Fellow at Somerville."

3. Mary Geach, "Introduction," in G. E. M. Anscombe, "Does Oxford Moral Philosophy Corrupt the Youth?", in *Human Life, Action and Ethics*, St. Andrews Studies in Philosophy and Public Policy, ed. Mary Geach and Luke Gormally (Exeter: Imprint Academic, 2005), Kindle edition.

SECONDARY IDEAS

KEY POINTS

- "Modern Moral Philosophy" has four main secondary ideas that together form the kernel of Anscombe's key objections to consequentialism.*

- She framed these key objections from the new perspective of virtue ethics*—an approach to moral philosophy that draws on the ethics of the ancient Greek philosopher Aristotle.

- Anscombe's account of intention and the description of actions has had a major impact upon action theory*—a subfield of philosophy that analyzes the nature of human action, inquiring into the mind, determinism,* and free will.

Other Ideas

There are four secondary themes in G. E. M. Anscombe's "Modern Moral Philosophy":

- The difference between foreseen consequences and intended consequences.
- The idea of an action as intended "under a description."
- The relationship between "ought" and "is."
- The return of rich concepts in ethics (like "virtue," "justice," and "truthfulness"), as opposed to blanket moral concepts such as "wrong," "ought," and the like.

Discussing the first of these themes, Anscombe points out that consequentialists such as the English philosopher Henry Sidgwick,* who subscribe to a moral philosophy that defines the moral value of an action solely in terms of its consequences, suppose that all *foreseen* consequences are *intended* consequences. Sidgwick "defines intention," Anscombe summarizes, "in such a way that one must be said to intend any foreseen consequences of one's voluntary action."[1] She argues that some foreseen consequences are not intended.

A second and related argument concerns whether an action is "intended under a description." By this phrase, Anscombe essentially means that an action is both intentional and intended as an action of injustice or murder or callousness. That is, it is both intended and the person performing the action has taken all relevant circumstances into account in his or her understanding of the action.

Anscombe also argues that it simply is not the case that an "ought" cannot be derived from an "is," as the eighteenth-century Scottish philosopher David Hume* had argued, and that it is easier to decide whether or not an action is unjust or callous than to decide whether it is "morally wrong." From the perspective of virtue ethics, however, it might be relatively easy to decide in a particular case whether an act was callous, for instance.

> "A man is responsible for the bad consequences of his bad actions, but gets no credit for the good ones; and contrariwise is not responsible for the bad consequences of good actions."
>
> ——G. E. M. Anscombe, "Modern Moral Philosophy"

Exploring the Ideas

Consequentialists argue that there is no difference between

choosing to act (or not act) with the *intention* of bringing about a particular intended consequence and choosing to act (or not act) with a *likelihood* of the same outcome.

Anscombe argues against this, illustrating her point with the example of a man who is solely responsible for a child's support and who must choose between two courses of action. He must either commit some unrelated injustice (like siphoning public money for a corrupt politician) under the threat of imprisonment, or he can refuse to engage in corruption and therefore be imprisoned by the politician, making it impossible for him to pay child support. According to the consequentialist view, he must weigh the "evil" of intentionally withdrawing child support (for, in consequentialism, all foreseen consequences are intended) against the evil of intentionally carrying out the unjust act.

Even if the unjust act is evil, the consequentialists would say that the man is justified in choosing to do it because this way he does not stop supporting the child. Anscombe says this is a problem: "A man is responsible for the bad consequences of his bad actions, but gets no credit for the good ones; and contrariwise is not responsible for the bad consequences of good actions."[2]

Anscombe goes on to discuss what she describes as action intended "under a description." By this, she essentially means that an action that is not sufficiently described or explained can be misunderstood morally. For example, destroying someone's home would normally be considered unjust. However, if you destroyed the home in order to prevent a fire from leaping from one village to another, the circumstances would change how we regarded the action in moral terms.

Consequentialists would argue, however, that in such a case it is the *consequences* that make an act of injustice morally right (in this case, of course, saving the other houses). But for Anscombe, intention makes a crucial difference. She argues that the nuanced description of the action would mean that the consequentialists are incorrect to say that injustice is rendered moral by its expected consequences:[3] burning a house down in order to prevent a fire from spreading just cannot be accurately described either as "injustice" or as "arson."

As we have seen, David Hume made a distinction between "is" and "ought." Anscombe argues that many ordinary factual statements imply an obligation—an "ought," in other words, is already present in the "is." If I owe someone money, I "ought" to pay the debt. So, if the butcher has delivered some meat to me, I owe money and ought to pay it. In other words, an analysis of justice shows that we *could* derive an "ought" from an "is." A statement of facts about relationships and institutions will contain the information necessary to decide on a just course of action.

Finally, Anscombe revives rich concepts based on virtue ethics—like justice and callousness—to replace "ought" and "right." For instance, choosing an abortion because you would no longer be able to afford to go on international holidays if you had a child would be an example of the vice of callousness, whereas choosing an abortion to save the life of the mother should not be called callous, regardless of any other ethical considerations.[4] Here she is in direct confrontation with the consequentialists, for whom any act might be permissible even if it is callous, provided it leads to the best foreseeable consequences.

Overlooked

As a very famous and relatively concise paper, "Modern Moral Philosophy" has been thoroughly examined, criticized, and interpreted. There is, though, one fairly brief comment in it that could be explored further.

Anscombe argues against Immanuel Kant's* approach to moral philosophy, dismissing it on the basis that it requires the concept of "legislating for oneself,"[5] which she considers nonsensical. When she was writing, Wittgenstein's* analysis of rule-following and of non-referential language use was a hot topic at Oxford and Cambridge universities, as was philosophy in "ordinary language"; Anscombe could assume a familiarity with these ideas. Kantian ethics,* however, had few followers.

Since then a new interest in Kant's ethics has emerged. The American virtue ethicist John Rawls's* influential *A Theory of Justice* (1971),[6] for instance, has brought Kant into the foreground again and so given Anscombe's arguments against him a wider audience. One scholar devotes an entire chapter to the legalistic conception of morality in his book on Anscombe's philosophy.[7] Anscombe herself wrote a further paper, "Rules, Rights and Promises,"[8] which develops the idea of the nature of obligation and committing oneself to a rule.

1. G. E. M. Anscombe, "Modern Moral Philosophy," *Philosophy* 33, no. 124 (1958): 9.

2. Anscombe, "Modern Moral Philosophy," 10.

3. Anscombe, "Modern Moral Philosophy," 13.

4. For a later development of this idea, see Rosalind Hursthouse, "Virtue Theory and Abortion," *Philosophy and Public Affairs* 20, no. 3 (1999): 238–42.

5. Anscombe, "Modern Moral Philosophy," 2.

6. John Rawls, *A Theory of Justice* (Cambridge, MA: Harvard University Press, 1971).

7. Roger Teichmann, *The Philosophy of Elizabeth Anscombe* (Oxford: Oxford University Press, 2008).

8. G. E. M. Anscombe, "Rules, Rights and Promises," in *Ethics, Religion and Politics* (Oxford: Basil Blackwell, 1981).

MODULE 7
ACHIEVEMENT

KEY POINTS

* Anscombe challenged consequentialism* and initiated a new program in moral philosophy: virtue ethics.*
* Virtue ethics has useful applications in government policy and medical ethics.*
* Anscombe's Christianity may have limited the paper's impact; some have dismissed it as an implicit argument for belief in God.

Assessing the Argument

In "Modern Moral Philosophy," G. E. M. Anscombe set out to reform her entire field of study. Her aims were threefold: to demonstrate that moral philosophy cannot be carried out "until we have an adequate philosophy of psychology, in which we are conspicuously lacking";[1] to show the problems inherent in "moral obligation"* and "ought" without belief in a divine legislator for morality; and to demonstrate that most English moral philosophers of the previous 75 years were ultimately the same—they all rejected Christianity and accepted consequentialism.

The essay was ambitious, but it did at least partially meet her aims. She succeeded in making a stinging criticism of consequentialism and Kantian ethics* on conceptual and moral grounds. The impact was immediate and many moral philosophers turned away from consequentialism.[2] She also raised enough contrasts between Aristotle's* moral philosophy and modern moral philosophy to revive an interest in virtue ethics. Anscombe's arguments in favor of the virtues were framed in an extremely engaging and interesting way, and this inspired other philosophers to follow her lead.

> *"'Modern Moral Philosophy'initiated the return to the idea of virtues as the central concepts needed by moral thought. It was enormously influential, turning firstly most of her Oxford generation, and then probably a majority of philosophers worldwide, against utilitarianism as a moral and political theory."*
>
> ——Simon Blackburn, "Against Anscombe,"
> *Times Literary Supplement*

Achievement in Context

Although Anscombe's "Modern Moral Philosophy" is primarily a philosophical text, it was also directly relevant to the political and social trends of the day. World War II* had seen virtually indiscriminate bombing of cities such as Dresden, Germany, resulting in huge civilian casualties on both sides. This had raised new moral questions because this mentality of "total war" meant that states justified the killing of civilians as a means of ending the war. Anscombe was appalled by this and it led to her questioning how such immoral thinking had come about. Her conclusion was that all the English moral philosophers from the Victorian philosopher Henry Sidgwick* to her day offered a justification. So Anscombe's arguments—that actions like intentionally killing innocent civilians can never be countenanced, whatever the supposed benefits—were radical in her day. As a result, some saw Anscombe as holding an extreme moral position.[3]

Anscombe was something of a revolutionary, given that she was one of the first philosophers in generations to propose that moral philosophy should return to virtue ethics. This meant that her essay was undervalued initially. However, because her thinking was so different from that of other moral philosophers of the time, her ideas had the benefit of novelty and gradually gathered support.

Limitations

A possible limitation of "Modern Moral Philosophy" is that it focused on Anscombe's contemporaries and their approach to moral philosophy. These included the philosophers R. M. Hare* and Patrick Nowell-Smith.* She essentially charges them with being unoriginal, stating that the differences between them and their predecessors are "of little importance."[4] While Anscombe was mainly challenging philosophers who are today mostly forgotten, she also included several important moral philosophers across the history of philosophy.

As a result, even if the argument about the similarity between consequentialist* philosophers seems dated, two other elements in the essay have a universal application. The first is the general analysis of the concept of morality and the relationship between moral obligation and a presumed divine legislative force. The second is the contrast between consequentialist approaches to ethics and virtue-based approaches.

One difficulty readers have found with Anscombe's essay is

its ambiguity about the relationship between religion and moral philosophy. Some philosophers have interpreted Anscombe as asserting that atheists cannot meaningfully use moral concepts and, as a result, have taken offence and largely ignored the essay. The British philosopher Simon Blackburn,* for instance, wrote: "If I feel I must avoid [words like "ought" and "obligation"] because I have been told that they are the private preserve of people who believe in divine law, then I have been hoodwinked and robbed."[5]

Most commentators, however, disagree with Blackburn. Anscombe scholars mostly claim that far from arguing against the possibility of secular moral philosophy, she wanted to help secular philosophers develop a conceptual framework for moral philosophy based on the virtues rather than on theological concepts.

---

1. G. E. M. Anscombe, "Modern Moral Philosophy," *Philosophy* 33, no. 124 (1958): 1.

2. Simon Blackburn, "Against Anscombe: Review of *Human Life, Action and Ethics*," *Times Literary Supplement*, September 30, 2005: 11–12.

3. This is reflected in the fact that only four other academics at Oxford University voted no to the awarding of an honorary doctorate to US president Harry S. Truman—the only world leader to have used the atomic bomb on human beings.

4. Anscombe, "Modern Moral Philosophy," 1.

5. Simon Blackburn, "Review of *Human Life, Action and Ethics*."

PLACE IN THE AUTHOR'S WORK

KEY POINTS

* Anscombe's writing was eclectic. She translated Wittgenstein's*
  Philosophical Investigations,[1] wrote *Intention*[2] (a seminal work
  in action theory),* and initiated the field of virtue ethics* with
  her paper "Modern Moral Philosophy."

* "Modern Moral Philosophy" is perhaps rivaled only by her book
  Intention in terms of its influence.

* Although many know her principally as Wittgenstein's
  translator, "Modern Moral Philosophy" marks Anscombe out as
  a philosopher in her own right.

Positioning

G. E. M. Anscombe's "Modern Moral Philosophy" was published
in 1958, when she was at the height of her philosophical career.
She had already published papers on varied topics and enjoyed a
prominent position in British philosophy. Anscombe had made
a very important translation of Wittgenstein's posthumously
published *Philosophical Investigations* in 1953, and Wittgenstein
remained perhaps the main influence on her thinking. Anscombe's
work in moral philosophy was essentially begun in earnest,
however, in 1957–8.

In 1957, Anscombe gave the radio address "Does Oxford
Moral Philosophy Corrupt the Youth?", in which she criticized the
way that moral philosophy was taught at Oxford University. The
following year, "Modern Moral Philosophy" was her philosophical

response to the perceived incoherence of contemporary moral systems.

Also in 1958 Anscombe published an important pamphlet, "Mr. Truman's Degree,"[3] which criticized both US President Harry S. Truman* for his bombing of civilians in the Japanese cities of Hiroshima and Nagasaki,* and Oxford University for subsequently honoring him with a degree. In fact, several of Anscombe's publications were connected in some way with World War II and its aftermath. Her very first publication—*The Justice of the Present War Examined*[4]—was written in 1939 on the subject of the morality of World War II. It is no overstatement to say that the policies of the Allies (the forces led by the United States and Britain) during World War II, bombing civilian targets, demanding unconditional surrender, and so on, were the most significant cause for Anscombe's reflection on moral philosophy. Her 1971 lecture "Causality and Determination"[5] was also a philosophically influential work.

> *"Elizabeth Anscombe was widely recognized as the most brilliant of Wittgenstein's students, as well as the pre-eminent translator and interpreter of his works. She was also an original and formidable philosopher in her own right, apparently able to reconcile a staunch Roman Catholicism with what she had learned from Frege, Aristotle, or Wittgenstein himself."*
>
> —— Simon Blackburn, "Against Anscombe,"
> *Times Literary Supplement*

Integration

Anscombe's life's work focused on the analysis of human action. She explored in technical detail what it was to "intend" to do something, writing *Intention* on this subject in 1957. This book, still considered one of the classics of twentieth-century philosophy, has been cited well over 3,000 times in scholarly articles and books. "Modern Moral Philosophy" fits within Anscombe's broader research examining the philosophy of how we *ought* to act—the question of moral obligation* (a requirement upon an individual to do something or refrain from doing something).

Anscombe's writings in the area of Roman Catholic* Christian morality cannot be ignored. Her works "Contraception and Chastity"[6] and "Action, Intention and 'Double Effect'"[7] have been influential both among Catholics and others. However, there is no real boundary between Anscombe's Catholic-informed ideas and her moral philosophy. For example, she shows her dismay at the contemporary loss of belief in natural moral law in "The Justice of the Present War Examined"—a work of Catholic moral theology. This idea was clearly a precursor to her argument in "Modern Moral Philosophy" that moral obligation had been stripped of its meaningful content by the rejection of Christianity.

Significance

The paper "Modern Moral Philosophy" is Anscombe's most influential work of moral philosophy. Perhaps only her book *Intention* can be said to have similar importance. The latter was published earlier and first brought Anscombe to prominence as a thinker.

One of the most important works in moral philosophy of the twentieth century, Anscombe's paper makes contributions in two principal areas. First, it initiated the virtue ethics movement in moral philosophy. Virtue ethics emphasizes qualities of character—like justice, courage, and wisdom—and their impact upon specific actions. The movement has included influential moral philosophers like Philippa Foot,* Alasdair MacIntyre,* and Rosalind Hursthouse.* Virtue ethics has gradually grown in prominence and nowadays enjoys widespread popularity among moral philosophers. An entire anthology was devoted to the virtue ethics movement in 2013—something that scholars trace back to Anscombe's article.[8] As the British moral philosopher Anthony O'Hear* summarizes: "In some quarters and in some ways, moral philosophy was changed by Anscombe's article and, in the opinion of many, for the better."[9]

Second, Anscombe's essay created significant interest in the question of moral obligation and divine command ethics.* Like Anscombe, divine command theorists maintain that there is a link between God and moral obligation. This view has been defended by the American philosophers Philip L. Quinn,* in *Divine Commands and Moral Requirements*,[10] and Robert Adams,* in *Finite and Infinite Goods.*[11] Adams has been influential, arguing that "obligation," "guilt," and "moral ought" are intrinsically social and therefore do require a divine being to whom we are accountable. This approach is very much in agreement with "Modern Moral Philosophy," as the social nature of these concepts can be accounted for by God.

1. Ludwig Wittgenstein, *Philosophical Investigations (Philosophische Untersuchungen) Eng. & Ger*, trans. G. E. M. Anscombe (Oxford: Basil Blackwell, 1953).

2. G. E. M. Anscombe, *Intention* (Oxford: Oxford University Press, 1957).

3. G. E. M. Anscombe, "Mr. Truman's Degree," in *Ethics, Religion and Politics* (Oxford: Basil Blackwell, 1981).

4. G. E. M. Anscombe, "The Justice of the Present War Examined," in *Ethics, Religion and Politics* (London: Basil Blackwell, 1981).

5. G. E. M. Anscombe, *Causality and Determination: An Inaugural Lecture* (Cambridge: Cambridge University Press, 1971).

6. G. E. M. Anscombe, *Contraception and Chastity* (London: Catholic Truth Society, 1975).

7. G. E. M. Anscombe, "Action, Intention and 'Double-Effect'," *Proceedings of the American Catholic Philosophical Association* 56 (1982): 12–25.

8. Daniel C. Russell, ed., *The Cambridge Companion to Virtue Ethics* (Cambridge: Cambridge University Press, 2013), 5.

9. Anthony O'Hear, "Preface," *Modern Moral Philosophy: Royal Institute of Philosophy Supplement 54*, ed. Anthony O'Hear (Cambridge: Cambridge University Press, 2004).

10. See Philip Quinn, *Divine Commands and Moral Requirements* (Oxford: Clarendon Library of Logic and Philosophy, 1978).

11. Robert Adams, *Finite and Infinite Goods: A Framework for Ethics* (Oxford: Oxford University Press, 2002).

SECTION 3
IMPACT

MODULE 9
THE FIRST RESPONSES

KEY POINTS

* Critics of "Modern Moral Philosophy" argue that moral obligation* is possible without divine authority, that there are defenses to her critique of consequentialism,* and that virtue ethics* needs to be explored further.

* Anscombe and her followers have maintained that distinguishing between foreseen and intended consequences is vital for clarity in moral philosophy; and that since virtue ethics does not rely on divine authority, it is a plausible ethical philosophy.

* Anscombe went on to develop a more nuanced view of the relationship between human actions and their foreseen consequences.

Criticism

One of the most widespread criticisms of G. E. M. Anscombe's "Modern Moral Philosophy" was that she had failed to argue persuasively the case that morality depended on a belief in God.

The philosopher Kai Nielsen,* for example, wrote an article criticizing Anscombe called "Some Remarks on the Independence of Morality from Religion."[1] He states, "No... knowledge that there is a God and that He issues commands, will by itself tell us what is good or what we ought to do."[2] This problem had been raised by the ancient Greek philosopher Plato* in his work *Euthyphro*,[3] and is summarized in the so-called *Euthyphro* dilemma: does God's command make an action right, or does God command certain actions because those actions are themselves already right? If the former is the case, then God could command heinous acts. If the latter, then God is not the basis of morality after all. Nielsen asserted that this question had been settled "since the *Euthyphro*."[4]

Another criticism came from consequentialists who set out to defend their moral theory. One example was the American philosopher Jonathan Bennett,* who argued that Anscombe's distinction between intended and merely foreseen consequences was morally irrelevant. Using examples from medical ethics, Bennett argued there is in fact no morally relevant difference between killing and allowing to die.[5] For example, a physician who stands by while someone goes into cardiac arrest cannot be excused for having simply "let the person die" rather than having "killed" the person. Positive reviews of Anscombe's work focused particularly on the revival of the virtues in moral philosophy.

> *"No... knowledge that there is a God and that He issues commands, will by itself tell us what is good or what we ought to do."*
> —— Kai Nielsen, "Some Remarks on the Independence of Morality from Religion"

Responses

Unfortunately, Anscombe did not respond to the charge that she had argued unpersuasively for the dependence of morality upon religion. There is in fact some contention among commentators as to whether she intended the paper to imply an argument for belief in God. While some continue to assert that she did,[6] the consensus view seems to be that it was not her primary intention to make such an argument—though that, of course, does not mean that she did not believe in such a link. The philosopher D. J. Richter* argues: "It is a mistake to conclude from [Anscombe's] argument that only a divine law or Aristotelian conception of ethics will do," because Anscombe herself explores such alternatives and finds them insufficient.[7] In short, Anscombe is open to other accounts of moral obligation; she just finds all of those accounts grossly lacking.

Anscombe's clearest response to criticism of "Modern Moral Philosophy" came in a very short note in the journal *Analysis* in response to Bennett's criticism of her distinction between acts and consequences.[8] She writes: "The nerve of Mr. Bennett's argument is that if A results from your not doing B, then A results from whatever you do instead of doing B. While there may be much to be said for this view, still it does not seem right on the face of it."[9] This exchange came at the very beginning of Anscombe's work on the relevance of intention to any philosophy of morality.

Conflict and Consensus

Although Anscombe seems to have held to her criticism of consequentialism to the last, she did seek to develop greater conceptual clarity about how to judge the morality of actions with bad foreseen but unintended consequences. Indeed, her talk "Action, Intention and 'Double-Effect'"[10] is a highly developed account of these concepts. Anscombe argues that if you foresee that deaths will almost certainly occur as a result of building a highway, you cannot reasonably be said to "intend" that foreseen consequence—and so you cannot be said to be guilty. She seems to have been spurred on to answer the criticisms of consequentialists like Bennett, who rejected her distinction between intended and foreseen consequences. He and others had done so on the basis of the charge that Anscombe was merely rehearsing the Roman Catholic* doctrine of double-effect: that you may not kill a person as a means to other (even good) ends, but that you may carry out an action that has the expected side effect of causing someone's death.

Anscombe responds in "Action, Intention, and 'Double-Effect'" that she is not a defender of "double-effect" but of the "principle of side-effects," writing: "'The principle of side-effects' is related to an absolute prohibition on seeking someone's death, either as an end or as means... It does not say when you may foreseeably cause death."[11] In short, Anscombe is interested *only* in showing that it is not always wrong to do something with the certain knowledge that someone's death will directly result. Her principle is meant to demonstrate what is different about the case of transplanting an organ from a living person and building a high-speed highway. They both result in the foreseen consequence of at least one person's death—but for her, the first is murder and the second is not.

---

1. Kai Nielsen, "Some Remarks on the Independence of Morality from Religion," *Mind* 70, no. 278 (1961): 175–86.

2. Nielsen, "Some Remarks," 175.

3. See Plato, *Euthyphro*, in *Readings in Ancient Greek Philosophy*, 2nd edition, ed. S. Marc Cohen and Patricia Curd, trans. C. D. C. Reeve (Indianapolis: Hackett Publishing, 2005), 97–114.

4. Nielsen, "Some Remarks," 175.

5. Jonathan Bennett, "Whatever the Consequences," *Analysis* 26, no. 2 (1966), 83–102.

6. See Thomas Pink, "Moral Obligation," in *Modern Moral Philosophy: Royal Institute of Philosophy Supplement 54*, ed. Anthony O'Hear (Cambridge: Cambridge University Press, 2004), 159–69; and Nielsen, "Some Remarks."

7. D. J. Richter, *Ethics after Anscombe: Post "Modern Moral Philosophy"* (Dordrecht: Springer Publishers, 2000), 29.

8. Bennett, "Whatever the Consequences."

9. G. E. M. Anscombe, "A Note on Mr. Bennett," *Analysis* 26, no. 6 (1966): 208.

10. G. E. M. Anscombe, "Action, Intention and 'Double-Effect,'" *Proceedings of the American Catholic Philosophical Association*, vol. 56 (1982): 12–25.

11. Anscombe, "Intention, Action and 'Double-Effect.'"

MODULE 10
THE EVOLVING DEBATE

KEY POINTS

• Virtue ethics* is a flourishing topic in moral philosophy and has opened the way for alternatives to consequentialism.*

• Virtue ethics sees the purpose of moral philosophy as being the analysis of virtues such as wisdom and temperance using psychology, literature, and history.

• "Modern Moral Philosophy" introduced a new subfield of moral philosophy, which continues to develop in a great number of directions.

Uses and Problems

G. E. M. Anscombe's "Modern Moral Philosophy" raised deep problems with the concept of "moral obligation"* and "moral ought." According to Anscombe, "The concepts of obligation, and duty... ought to be jettisoned if this is psychologically possible."[1]

This idea did not appeal to those philosophers who followed Kantian ethics* and utilitarianism* (for whom Anscombe coined the term "consequentialists"). Both of these theories rely upon a secular account of "moral obligation" and Anscombe was questioning whether such a concept had any meaning.

As the philosopher Simon Blackburn* has since conceded, the text was "enormously influential, turning firstly most of her Oxford generation, and then probably a majority of philosophers worldwide, against utilitarianism as a moral and political theory."[2] As a result, a search began for an understanding of morality in the tradition of virtue ethics. Anscombe had ignited interest in virtue ethics generally and in the ethics of Aristotle* specifically.

> "Elizabeth Anscombe's 'Modern Moral Philosophy'... has played a significant part in the development of so-called 'virtue ethics,' which has burgeoned over the last three decades in particular."
>
> —— Roger Crisp, "Does Modern Moral Philosophy Rest on a Mistake?"

Schools of Thought

This new approach to ethics has spawned a great deal of research in the fields of virtue ethics and experimental moral psychology. Although Anscombe herself did not pursue a full conceptual account of virtue ethics, her work encouraged many other philosophers to try to forge a way of using the virtues in contemporary moral philosophy.

Anscombe's close friend and fellow philosopher Philippa Foot* wrote *Virtues and Vices*[3] and *Natural Goodness*,[4] two classics in virtue ethics. Peter Geach,* Anscombe's husband, also wrote a book called *The Virtues* in 1974. Both Foot and Geach argue for a "naturalistic" account of the virtues—one grounded in human biology and sociology rather than "moral obligation." As Geach famously argued: "Men are benefited by virtues as bees are by having stings."[5] In other words, virtues are a normal part of the character of normal human beings; we are defective without them and cannot flourish. Philippa Foot argues in her 2001 book *Natural Goodness* that human biology can provide grounds for virtue ethics.[6]

In addition to the virtue ethics movement in moral philosophy, Anscombe's essay also impacted the field of Christian ethics, or moral theology ("theology" refers to the systematic study of religious concepts, usually conducted through the analysis of Scripture). The theologians Stanley Hauerwas* and William Frankena,* for instance, began developing Christian interpretations of the virtues in the 1970s. Hauerwas's work, in particular, has assimilated the use of virtue ethics in Christian theology and life.[7]

In Current Scholarship

The contemporary virtue ethics movement is perhaps at the most prolific moment in its history; in 2013, Cambridge University Press produced an entire anthology devoted to virtue ethics.[8] One cannot overstate Anscombe's impact, and many questions addressed in the current movement can be traced back to her writings on the medieval* and ancient* proponents of virtue ethics.

Anscombe's comments on the ethics of Aristotle and the medieval theologian Thomas Aquinas* were significant contributions. One of the most important figures in contemporary virtue ethics is Alasdair MacIntyre,* whose book *After Virtue* was published in 1981.[9] In it, MacIntyre takes up several of Anscombe's themes, including a detailed conceptual account of the virtues.[10] MacIntyre is also author of *Dependent Rational Animals*, which analyzes the impact of human biology on the way we should think about the virtues and moral development.[11]

Rosalind Hursthouse* of the University of Auckland is another leading figure in virtue ethics; she made a vital contribution to virtue ethics with her 2001 book *On Virtue Ethics*. Hursthouse argues that virtue ethics can produce what she calls "v-rules": rules centered on virtues and vices.[12] So if one comes to understand that having an abortion to further one's career would be a callous act, it follows that one ought not to have an abortion. These rules make virtue ethics a "normative" moral theory and therefore a rival to consequentialism and Kantian ethics.

The most recent proponents of virtue ethics are Martha Nussbaum* and the notable Indian economist Amartya Sen.* Martha Nussbaum is an American philosopher who specializes in ancient philosophy and literature. She produced several important works in moral psychology that emphasized the importance of emotions such as love, compassion, grief, shame, and disgust in ethical thinking. She also worked with Amartya Sen to develop the "capabilities" approach to welfare economics, focusing on the capabilities central to living a flourishing life. Nussbaum listed 10, including the capacity to form emotional attachments, to reason, to play, and to be healthy. This approach has been useful in comparing and measuring international development, and was instrumental in forming the Human Development Index—an international measure for developmental welfare.

---

1. G. E. M. Anscombe, "Modern Moral Philosophy," *Philosophy* 33, no. 124 (1958): 1.

2. Simon Blackburn, "Against Anscombe: Review of *Human Life, Action and Ethics*," *Times Literary Supplement*, September 30, 2005: 11–12.

3. Philippa Foot, *Virtues and Vices and Other Essays in Moral Philosophy* (Berkeley and Los Angeles:

University of California Press, 1978).

4. Philippa Foot, *Natural Goodness* (Oxford: Oxford University Press, 2001).

5. Peter Geach, *The Virtues* (Cambridge: Cambridge University Press, 1977), vii.

6. Foot, *Natural Goodness*, 51.

7. Stanley Hauerwas, *Character and the Christian Life* (San Antonio, TX: Trinity University Press, 1975).

8. Daniel C. Russell, ed., *The Cambridge Companion to Virtue Ethics* (Cambridge: Cambridge University Press, 2013).

9. Alasdair MacIntyre, *After Virtue*, 3rd revised edition (London: Duckworth, 2007).

10. MacIntyre, *After Virtue,* 191.

11. Alasdair MacIntyre, *Dependent Rational Animals* (London: Duckworth, 1999).

12. Rosalind Hursthouse, *On Virtue Ethics* (Oxford: Oxford University Press, 2001), 36–42.

IMPACT AND INFLUENCE TODAY

KEY POINTS

* "Modern Moral Philosophy" helps to define moral philosophy by dividing it into consequentialism,* Kantian ethics,* and virtue ethics.*

* It still poses the problem for Kantian ethics that Kant's* concept of legislating for oneself—passing and enforcing one's own "laws"—is incoherent.

* Anscombe targeted consequentialist and Kantian ethics as immoral.

Position

One significant contribution that G. E. M. Anscombe's "Modern Moral Philosophy" made to the contemporary debate is her coining of the term "consequentialism." Until her paper, a host of moral theories had been grouped under the term "utilitarianism"* (a moral and political philosophy that judges an action according to its capacity to cause the greatest happiness for the greatest number).

Her second main contribution was the raising of huge questions about moral obligation* (a requirement of an individual to do something or refrain from doing something); this has invited further research, including questioning whether ethics should be understood in "naturalist" or "nonnaturalist" terms. Those who argue for naturalist ethics believe there is an essential similarity between ethical judgments and everyday value judgments: if the farmer produces good vegetables and sustains his land, then he is a good farmer. Nonnaturalists argue that there is a gap between facts and values, so that the property of "goodness" or "rightness" must be a nonnatural property of certain actions. For instance, it does not follow from the fact that football brings pleasure (according to nonnaturalists) that watching football is morally right. The pleasure that you experience must have the additional property of "goodness."

Finally, the essay divided the contemporary field of ethics into three main categories: consequentialism, Kantian ethics, and virtue ethics. Indeed, the paper is still regularly cited in a huge number of books and articles published on virtue ethics, and is therefore a key starting point for any student seeking to understand moral philosophy.

> *"Philosophers like Elizabeth Anscombe and Philippa Foot… advocated a turn to virtue ethics as the logical conclusion of the contemporary quest to clarify and ground the central concepts of ethics."*
>
> —— Daniel C. Russell, *The Cambridge Companion to Virtue Ethics*

Interaction

"Modern Moral Philosophy" remains important today as the first major objection to consequentialism with enough depth to be able to initiate an alternative. Although the essay had a number of impacts on consequentialism, three stand out.

First, Anscombe argued that consequentialism implies that no

131

kind of action is ruled out absolutely. Since it is at least possible that convicting and killing the innocent could have beneficial consequences, for example, a consequentialist can never simply prohibit such an injustice.

Second, Anscombe persuasively argued that although consequentialism, especially in its utilitarian forms, was entirely based on the concept of "pleasure," it cannot even give a full account of what pleasure is. As a result, consequentialists today often focus instead on the satisfaction of preferences, rather than the realization of pleasure.

Third, there remains considerable debate about the distinction between intended and merely foreseen consequences. Anscombe wrote on this subject again in "Action, Intention and 'Double-Effect'" in 1981, when she presented a detailed defense of the importance of distinguishing intended from foreseen consequences.[1] Many consequentialists, however, have maintained that there is not a morally significant difference between the two. The philosophy professor Jonathan Bennett, an early critic of Anscombe, explores the distinction further in "Morality and Consequences"[2] and *The Act Itself* (1995).[3]

The Continuing Debate

Anscombe argued against consequentialists "from Sidgwick to the present day."[4] One modern defender of consequentialism is the Australian philosopher Peter Singer,* who systematically defends Sidgwick in *The Point of View of the Universe: Sidgwick and Contemporary Ethics*.[5] The continued relevance of Sidgwick—

for even the most prominent consequentialist philosophers like Singer—demonstrates the insight of Anscombe's claim that the publication of Sidgwick's *Methods of Ethics* (1874) was a watershed in the history of ethics.[6]

Unlike previous moral philosophers, Sidgwick and his followers deny that any kind of action is ruled out categorically. So, to take one of Peter Singer's favorite examples, killing an infant is not prohibited—provided that the infant is disabled and his parents want him killed. This is because, according to Singer, infants do not possess rational self-awareness, or personhood. He concludes in his book *Practical Ethics* that, therefore, "Reasons for not killing persons do not apply to newborn infants."[7] Anscombe's moral arguments become particularly relevant here as current consequentialists consider an act as heinous as infanticide in terms of a mere cost–benefit analysis.

Anscombe also targets Kantian ethics in her paper. The Kantian approach has seen a major upturn since the publication of "Modern Moral Philosophy." Perhaps the foremost Kantian moral philosopher is Christine Korsgaard* of Harvard University, whose 1996 book *The Sources of Normativity* is a systematic defense of her position. Although Anscombe said that the idea that one can legislate for oneself is absurd, Korsgaard argues that self-reflection gives humans the possibility of becoming their own moral authorities.[8] Since "authority" is normally the province of a greater power over a lesser, however, it is unclear exactly how Korsgaard's account overturns Anscombe's argument in "Modern Moral Philosophy."

1. G. E. M. Anscombe, *Human Life, Action and Ethics*, ed. by Mary Geach and Luke Gormally (Exeter: Imprint Academic, 2005), Kindle edition.

2. Jonathan Bennett, "Morality and Consequences," in *The Tanner Lectures on Human Values*, vol. 2, ed. by Sterling McMurrin (Salt Lake City: University of Utah Press, 1981), 110–11.

3. Jonathan Bennett, *The Act Itself* (New York: Oxford University Press, 1995), 194–225.

4. G. E. M. Anscombe, "Modern Moral Philosophy," *Philosophy* 33, no. 124 (1958): 1.

5. Katarzyna de Lazari-Radek and Peter Singer, *The Point of View of the Universe: Sidgwick and Contemporary Ethics* (Oxford: Oxford University Press, 2014).

6. Henry Sidgwick, *Methods of Ethics*, 7th edition (Indianapolis: Hackett, 1981).

7. Peter Singer, *Practical Ethics* (Cambridge: Cambridge University Press, 1979), 124.

8. Christine Korsgaard, *The Sources of Normativity* (Cambridge: Cambridge University Press, 1996), 19–20.

MODULE 12
WHERE NEXT?

KEY POINTS

* "Modern Moral Philosophy" will continue to be an important text because it provides both strong arguments and an alternative to consequentialism* and Kantian ethics.*
* The essay reinvigorated virtue ethics* as an approach to moral philosophy.
* Research on virtue ethics will continue to expand in fruitful directions in the future.

Potential

Having helped transform moral philosophy in the twentieth and twenty-first centuries, G. E. M. Anscombe's "Modern Moral Philosophy" will remain an influential text. The essay continues to provide a clear and well-argued critique of consequentialist and Kantian moral philosophy. It will continue to be a standard essay for philosophy students because it raises deep questions about the nature of moral obligation,* it contrasts the theories of some of the most influential moral thinkers in the history of philosophy, and its publication was a watershed moment in the history of the virtue ethics tradition in moral philosophy.

The greatest potential for the text in the future lies in its capacity to inspire philosophers to pursue enquiry into virtue ethics. There are indications that virtue ethics, while remaining a minority view, will continue to rise in popularity and academic rigor. Specifically, virtue ethics is beginning to be appropriated in areas like applied ethics* (the subfield of moral philosophy that focuses on applying moral principles to concrete situations) and its subfield of bioethics* (which inquires into medical and environmental ethical issues) and to political philosophy. The year 2013 saw the publication of an anthology of "applied virtue ethics" called *Virtues in Action: New Essays in Applied Virtue Ethics*,[1] for example. Topics cover a range of issues including "The Virtues of Honourable Business Executives" and "Humility and Environmental Virtue Ethics."

Similarly, the *Cambridge Companion to Virtue Ethics*[2] was published for the first time in 2013—as were dozens of articles and books on the subject of the virtues.

> "In some quarters and in some ways, moral philosophy was changed by Anscombe's article and, in the opinion of many, for the better."
>
> —— Anthony O'Hear, *Modern Moral Philosophy*

Future Directions

Although "Modern Moral Philosophy" lays out a new direction for moral philosophy, certain aspects need to be developed—among them a philosophical analysis of moral psychology, accounts of the virtues, and an understanding of "above all, human flourishing."[3] These themes continue to be developed in fascinating directions. The American philosopher Martha Nussbaum,* for instance, is a contemporary virtue ethicist who writes about human flourishing. She has produced several important works on moral psychology that emphasize the importance of such emotions as love, compassion, grief, shame, and disgust in ethical thinking. She worked with Amartya Sen,* winner of the Nobel Prize in economics in 1998, to develop the "capabilities" approach to welfare economics that defines welfare in terms of the capabilities central to living a flourishing life.

Nussbaum listed, among others, the capability to form emotional attachments, to reason, to play, and to be healthy as essential capabilities. The capabilities approach has been useful in comparing and measuring international development and was instrumental in forming the Human Development Index, an international measure for developmental welfare. Perhaps this direction of the virtue ethics movement—human flourishing and human virtues in relation to politics and economics—will prove one of the most fruitful.

Summary

"Modern Moral Philosophy" remains one of the most important texts in twentieth-century moral philosophy. In it, G. E. M. Anscombe's keen analytical eye ranges over consequentialism, Kantian ethics, and contractualism,* and finds each of them either immoral or conceptually incoherent.

Consequentialism depends upon a questionable concept of "pleasure," she finds, and leads to immoral conclusions (consequentialists must be open, for example, to the possibility that condemning the innocent to death is the "right" thing to do—provided it has some positive consequence overall). This view, says Anscombe, is characteristic of someone who "has a corrupt mind."[4] Kantian ethics depends upon the concept of legislating for oneself, which she finds incoherent. Contractualism makes morality dependent on whatever the majority happens to believe at any one time, which again leads to disastrous moral conclusions.

Additionally, Anscombe raises questions about the nature of "moral" words like "obligation," "ought," and "right," and argues that the concepts as used by contemporary philosophers do not make sense as they have no belief in a divine lawmaker. This is because the concepts are intrinsically social ones—you are commanded to do something or prohibited from doing something by a greater power. However, Anscombe pushes her readers to seek an alternative way of discussing good and bad human action. This method, she argues, will depend upon richer concepts, like "justice," "virtue," and "charity." This resulted in the development of the virtue ethics movement, which has become influential in moral philosophy over the past 40 years.

These aspects make "Modern Moral Philosophy" one of the most important essays in the history of moral philosophy. Every reader will benefit from the questions and arguments Anscombe raises in a work that provides a wonderful introduction to those wishing to understand the state of moral philosophy from the middle of the twentieth century to the present day.

---

1. Michael W. Austin, ed., *Virtues in Action: New Essays in Applied Virtue Ethics* (Basingstoke: Palgrave Macmillan, 2013).

2. Daniel C. Russell, ed., *The Cambridge Companion to Virtue Ethics* (Cambridge: Cambridge University Press, 2013).

3. G. E. M. Anscombe, "Modern Moral Philosophy," *Philosophy* 33, no. 124 (1958): 1–16.

4. Anscombe, "Modern Moral Philosophy," 14.

 GLOSSARY OF TERMS

1. **Action theory:** a subfield of philosophy that analyzes the nature of human action. It involves questions about the mind, determinism, and free will.

2. **Analytic philosophy:** a philosophical set of methods that focuses on detailed analysis of concepts and language. It is the dominant method in Britain and the United States, and its roots were in late nineteenth- and early twentieth-century philosophy at the University of Cambridge.

3. **Ancient:** in philosophy, the period of ancient Greek and Roman philosophy was from roughly 400 B.C.E. to 200 C.E. Important figures include Plato, Aristotle, and Cicero.

4. **Applied ethics:** the subfield of moral philosophy that focuses on applying moral principles to concrete situations. It contains further subdivisions such as "bioethics" and the ethics of technology.

5. **Aristotelian approach to ethics:** a version of ethical theory that draws substantially from the ancient Greek philosopher Aristotle. Aristotle based ethics on the virtues, as well as the concept of *eudaimonia* (roughly, happiness).

6. **Bioethics:** a subfield of moral philosophy that focuses on medical ethics, ethics of the environment, and ethics of animal treatment. It was developed largely in the 1960s.

7. **Bombing of Hiroshima and Nagasaki:** in 1945, the United States—under the authority of President Harry S. Truman—bombed the major Japanese cities of Hiroshima and Nagasaki in order to bring an end to World War II. The act remains controversial and is considered by many an act of mass murder of civilians.

8. **Categorical imperative:** the imperative that applies in all cases; the theory that one should always act in accordance with maxims that one can choose as a universal law.

9. **Consequentialism:** a term coined by Anscombe in "Modern Moral Philosophy" that now has broad currency. It refers to any moral philosophy that defines the moral value of an action solely in terms of its consequences.

10. **Contractualism:** a theory of morality that proposes that an implicit contract exists between members of a community and that this contract grounds moral obligation.

139

11. **Deontology:** a moral philosophy focusing on duties. Kant's ethical philosophy is the prime example; this argues that every rational being has the duty to obey the categorical imperative.

12. **Determinism:** the philosophical view that every event in the universe (including every human action) is causally determined by the previous state of the physical universe.

13. **Divine command ethics/Divine law ethics:** a theory of moral obligation that asserts that actions are obligatory which have the property of being commanded by God.

14. **Ethical anti-realism:** the thesis that moral facts do not exist. While consequentialism is the thesis that consequences alone have moral value, one can arguably be a consequentialist and be either an ethical anti-realist or a realist.

15. **Ethical intuitionism:** the view that individuals know moral truths because they have direct access to moral facts through a faculty of intuition. It was developed by the philosophers Henry Sidgwick and G. E. Moore.

16. **Ethics:** the subdiscipline of philosophy that focuses on the theoretical and practical aspects of morality. It seeks primarily to answer the questions "What is the nature of the good life?" and "How ought we to live?"

17. **Kantian ethics:** a theory of moral obligation (sometimes called "deontology") that asserts that one's obligation is to act in ways one would at the same time prescribe as a universal moral law.

18. **Law conception of ethics:** any conception of ethics that uses legalistic language such as "obligation," "ought," "right," and "permitted." This conception of ethics has its roots in early Christian belief in divine law authorized by God.

19. **Medical ethics:** a subfield of applied ethics that focuses on the ethics of medicine. Central themes include patient and physician autonomy, abortion, euthanasia, and medical testing on human subjects.

20. **Medieval:** The medieval period of philosophy was roughly from 400 to 1400 C.E. In the West, it was characterized most importantly by Christian philosophical and theological reflection.

21. **Metaphysics:** the study of the ultimate nature of reality.

22. **Moral obligation:** refers in philosophy to a requirement upon an individual to do something or refrain from doing something. A moral obligation is normally believed to override other requirements—either self-interest or social expectations.

23. **Moral philosophy:** another term for ethics.

24. **Naturalistic fallacy:** a concept developed by the philosopher G. E. Moore. Moore argued that, for any natural property of a thing, one could question whether that property was good or bad; therefore to identify goodness itself with such a property is a mistake.

25. **Progressivism:** a social and political view that makes "progress" the highest political aim. It is linked with consequentialism in ethics.

26. **Roman Catholicism:** a form of Christianity that dates back to the lives of Jesus Christ's first followers. The world's largest Christian denomination, Roman Catholicism has a tradition of producing world-leading philosophers.

27. **Utilitarianism:** a moral and political philosophy that rates the best action to be the one that produces the greatest happiness in the greatest number. The theory's greatest advocates were social and legal reformers Jeremy Bentham and John Stuart Mill.

28. **Victorian period:** the time of Queen Victoria's reign in Great Britain: 1837–1901. It was characterized by British imperialism and industrialization.

29. **Virtue ethics:** an approach to normative ethics that identifies the good life in terms of attaining, and acting in accord with, virtues such as justice, wisdom, and generosity.

30. **The virtues:** dispositions of character that are expressed in human action. They include justice, temperance, and courage, and they form the core of the virtue ethics approach to moral philosophy.

31. **World War II (1939–45):** the single greatest armed conflict in human history, World War II engaged the Allies (for example, Great Britain, the United States, the Soviet Union, and China) against the Axis Powers (Nazi Germany, Italy, and Japan). It pushed forward one of the world's most rapid periods of modernization.

1. **Robert Adams (b. 1937)** is an American philosopher who specializes in moral philosophy and metaphysics. Adams's most important contributions have been to the divine command theory of obligation, namely his *Finite and Infinite Goods* (1999).

2. **Thomas Aquinas, also known as Tommaso d'Aquino (1225–74)** was a particularly influential theologian, philosopher, and educator of the medieval period.

3. **Aristotle (384–322 B.C.E.)** was an ancient Greek philosopher who first coined the term "ethics." His ethical philosophy was based on perfecting the virtues by reaching the golden mean between extremes of behavior.

4. **Jonathan Bennett (b. 1930)** is professor emeritus in the philosophy department at Syracuse University. His specialisms are philosophy of mind and the history of philosophy.

5. **Jeremy Bentham (1748–1832)** was an English philosopher and social reformer regarded as the pioneer of the philosophical school of utilitarianism. He argued that an action's morality should be judged by how much pleasure it produced and how much pain it prevented or alleviated.

6. **Simon Blackburn (b. 1944)** is a prominent British philosopher and retired Bertrand Russell Professor of Philosophy at the University of Cambridge. His books, in the school of Hume's philosophy, include *Spreading the Word* (1984) and *Essays in Quasi-realism* (1993).

7. **Philippa Foot (1920–2010)** was an English philosopher whose work chiefly refocused professional ethical philosophical discussion around virtues and vices as opposed to consequences or duties.

8. **William Frankena (1908–94)** was an influential American philosopher who taught at the University of Michigan. His specialism was moral philosophy, and his most influential work was *Ethics* (1963).

9. **Peter Geach (1916–2013)** was an English philosopher who specialized in logic and moral philosophy. His most notable works are *The Virtues* (1977) and "Ascriptivism" (1960).

10. **R. M. Hare (1919–2002)** was a key English moral philosopher of the twentieth century. A utilitarian theorist, his most important work is *The Language of Morals* (1952).

11. **Stanley Hauerwas (b. 1940)** is a Christian ethicist and the Gilbert T. Rowe Professor Emeritus of Divinity at Duke University. His main works are *Character and the Christian Life* (1975) and *The Peaceable Kingdom* (1983).

12. **David Hume (1711–76)** was an influential Scottish empiricist philosopher who authored *Dialogues Concerning Natural Religion* (1779) and *An Enquiry Concerning the Principles of Morals* (1751). His moral theory sought to ground ethics in the human sentiments or feelings.

13. **Rosalind Hursthouse (b. 1943)** is professor of philosophy at the University of Auckland, New Zealand. She is a prominent neo-Aristotelian virtue ethicist, whose major works are "Virtue Theory and Abortion" (1991) and *On Virtue Ethics* (1999).

14. **Immanuel Kant (1724–1804)** was one of the most influential philosophers of the period of European intellectual history known as the Enlightenment (roughly 1750–1900, characterized by dramatic revolutions in the sciences and in philosophy, where increasing confidence was placed in the power of reason). He was the author of many works, including *Critique of Pure Reason* (1781) and *Groundwork of the Metaphysics of Morals* (1785), and he argued that ethics ought to be grounded in rationality.

15. **Christine Korsgaard (b. 1952)** is professor of philosophy at Harvard University. A Kantian moral philosopher, her most important work is *The Sources of Normativity* (1996).

16. **Alasdair MacIntyre (b. 1929)** is a Scottish moral philosopher who has held teaching positions at several major US universities. His most important works are in virtue ethics and include *After Virtue* (1981) and *Dependent Rational Animals:Why Human Beings Need the Virtues* (1999).

17. **John Stuart Mill (1806–73)** was an English philosopher and legal reformer who studied under Jeremy Bentham and developed his theory of utilitarianism.

18. **G. E. Moore (1873–1958)** was an English philosopher famous in Cambridge for an argument called the "naturalistic fallacy," purporting to show that value terms like "good" are not reducible to natural terms like feelings of pleasure.

19. **Kai Nielsen (b. 1926)** is a moral philosopher and professor emeritus at the University of Calgary. His books include *Ethics without God* (1971).

20. **Patrick Nowell-Smith (1914–2006)** was an English moral philosopher and utilitarian. His most important work is *Ethics* (1956).

21. **Martha Nussbaum (b. 1947)** is the Ernst Freund Distinguished Service Professor of Law and Ethics at the University of Chicago. She is author of *The Fragility of Goodness* (1986) and *Upheavals of Thought:The Intelligence of Emotions* (2001), and she seeks to complement Kantian ethics with Aristotle.

22. **Anthony O'Hear** is a British philosopher, professor at Buckingham University, and director of the Royal Institute for Philosophy. His works include *After Progress* (1999).

23. **Plato (c. 427–347 B.C.E.)** was one of the most important philosophers in history. A disciple of Socrates, his dialogues cover most of the basic issues across the entire range of philosophical discourse—covering ethics, politics, knowledge, and God.

24. **Philip L. Quinn (1940–2004)** was a philosopher and theologian, noted as a scholar of the philosophy of physics and of ethics.

25. **John Rawls (1921–2002)** was a Harvard University professor and one of the most influential political philosophers of the twentieth century. His masterpiece, *A Theory of Justice*, published in 1971, forms the foundation of much contemporary liberal political theory.

26. **D. J. Richter** is a moral philosopher at Virginia Military Institute and author of *Ethics after Anscombe* (2000) and *Anscombe's Moral Philosophy* (2011).

27. **Amartya Sen (b. 1933)** is an Indian economist and Nobel laureate. He introduced the concept of welfare economics based on the capabilities approach that is influenced by virtue ethics.

28. **Henry Sidgwick (1838–1900)** was an English utilitarian philosopher and

economist who promoted higher education for women. He is no longer widely known.

29. **Peter Singer (b. 1946)** is an Australian moral philosopher. He is perhaps the world's foremost utilitarian, and his books include *Practical Ethics* (1979) and *Animal Liberation: A New Ethics for Our Treatment of Animals* (1975).

30. **Harry S. Truman (1884–1972)** was the 33rd president of the United States, 1945–53. He forced the surrender of the Japanese in World War II by authorizing the nuclear devastation of Hiroshima and Nagasaki, which resulted in the deaths of hundreds of thousands of people.

31. **Ludwig Wittgenstein (1889–1951)** was an Austrian-born philosopher who worked mainly in England. His posthumously published master work *Philosophical Investigations* (1953) was collated and translated from German to English by his star student Elizabeth Anscombe and was enormously influential in British twentieth-century philosophy.

 **WORKS CITED**

1. Adams, Robert. *Finite and Infinite Goods: A Framework for Ethics*. Oxford: Oxford University Press, 2002.

2. Anscombe, G. E. M. "Action, Intention and 'Double-Effect'." *Proceedings of the American Catholic Philosophical Association* 56 (1982): 12–25.

3. ———. *Causality and Determination: An Inaugural Lecture*. Cambridge: Cambridge University Press, 1971.

4. ———. *Contraception and Chastity*. London: Catholic Truth Society, 1975.

5. ———. *Ethics, Religion and Politics*. Oxford: Basil Blackwell, 1981.

6. ———. *Human Life, Action and Ethics*. St. Andrews Studies in Philosophy and Public Policy. Edited by Mary Geach and Luke Gormally. Exeter: Imprint Academic, 2005. Kindle edition.

7. ———. *Intention*. Oxford: Basil Blackwell, 1957.

8. ———. "Modern Moral Philosophy." *Philosophy* 33, no. 124 (1958): 1–19.

9. ———. "A Note on Mr. Bennett." *Analysis* 26, no. 6 (1966): 208.

10. Aristotle. *Nicomachean Ethics*. Edited and translated by Roger Crisp. Cambridge: Cambridge University Press, 2014.

11. Austin, Michael W., ed. *Virtues in Action: New Essays in Applied Virtue Ethics*. Basingstoke: Palgrave Macmillan, 2013.

12. Ayer, A. J. *Language, Truth and Logic*. London: Victor Gollancz, 1936.

13. Bennett, Jonathan. *The Act Itself*. New York: Oxford University Press, 1995.

14. ———. "Morality and Consequences." In *The Tanner Lectures on Human Values*, vol. 2, edited by Sterling McMurrin, 110–11. Salt Lake City: University of Utah Press, 1981.

15. ———. "Whatever the Consequences." *Analysis* 26, no. 2 (1966): 83–102.

16. Bentham, Jeremy. *An Introduction to the Principles of Morals and Legislation*. Oxford: Clarendon Press, 1907.

17. Blackburn, Simon. "Against Anscombe: Review of *Human Life, Action and Ethics*." *Times Literary Supplement*, September 30, 2005: 11–12.

18. Conradi, Peter J. *Iris Murdoch: A Life*. London: HarperCollins, 2002.

19. Crisp, Roger. "Does Moral Philosophy Rest on a Mistake?", *Royal Institute of Philosophy Supplement* 54 (March 2004): 75–93. Accessed October 7, 2015. doi: 10.1017/S1358246100008456.

20. Driver, Julia. "Gertrude Elizabeth Margaret Anscombe." In *Stanford Encyclopedia of Philosophy* (Winter 2014 edition), edited by Edward N. Zalta. Accessed October 6, 2015. http://plato.stanford.edu/entries/anscombe/.

21. ———. "The History of Utilitarianism." In *Stanford Encyclopedia of Philosophy* (Winter 2014 edition), edited by Edward N. Zalta. Accessed October 6, 2015. http://plato.stanford.edu/entries/utilitarianism-history/.

22. Foot, Philippa. *Natural Goodness*. Oxford: Oxford University Press, 2001.

23. ———. *Virtue and Vices and Other Essays in Moral Philosophy*. Berkeley and Los Angeles: University of California Press, 1978.

24. Frankena, William K. "The Ethics of Love Conceived as an Ethics of Virtue." *Journal of Religious Ethics* 1 (Fall 1973): 21–36.

25. Fricker, Miranda. *Epistemic Injustice: Power and the Ethics of Knowing*. Oxford: Oxford University Press, 2007.

26. Geach, Peter T. *The Virtues*. Cambridge: Cambridge University Press, 1977.

27. Hauerwas, Stanley. *Character and the Christian Life*. San Antonio, TX: Trinity University Press, 1975.

28. ———. "Obligation and Virtue Once More." *Journal of Religious Ethics* 3, no.1 (Spring 1975): 27–44.

29. Hume, David. *Treatise of Human Nature.* Edited by L. A. Selby-Bigge and P. H. Nidditch. 2nd edition. Oxford: Oxford University Press, 1978.

30. Hursthouse, Rosalind. *Beginning Lives*. Oxford: Basil Blackwell in association with the Open University, 1987.

31. ———. *On Virtue Ethics*. Oxford: Oxford University Press: 2001.

32. ———. "Virtue Theory and Abortion." *Philosophy and Public Affairs* 20, no. 3

(1991): 223–46.

33. Korsgaard, Christine. *The Sources of Normativity*. Cambridge: Cambridge University Press, 1996.

34. Lazari-Radek, Katarzyna de and Peter Singer. *The Point of View of the Universe: Sidgwick and Contemporary Ethics*. Oxford: Oxford University Press, 2014.

35. MacIntyre, Alasdair. *After Virtue*. 3rd revised edition. London: Duckworth, 2007.

36. ———. *Dependent Rational Animals*. London: Duckworth, 1999.

37. Murdoch, Iris. *The Sovereignty of Good*. London: Routledge & Kegan Paul, 1970.

38. Nielsen, Kai. "Some Remarks on the Independence of Morality from Religion." *Mind* 70, no. 278 (1961): 175–86.

39. Nietzsche, Friedrich Wilhelm. *Beyond Good and Evil: Prelude to a Philosophy of the Future*. Translated by R. J. Hollingdale. Harmondsworth: Penguin, 1990.

40. ———. *On the Genealogy of Morals: A Polemic: By Way of Clarification and Supplement to My Last Book Beyond Good and Evil*. Translated by Douglas Smith. Oxford: Oxford University Press, 1996.

41. Nussbaum, Martha. *Upheavals of Thought: The Intelligence of Emotions*. Cambridge: Cambridge University Press, 2001.

42. O'Hear, Anthony, ed. *Modern Moral Philosophy: Royal Institute of Philosophy Supplement 54*. Cambridge: Cambridge University Press, 2004.

43. Pink, Thomas. "Moral Obligation." in *Modern Moral Philosophy: Royal Institute of Philosophy Supplement 54*, ed. Anthony O'Hear. Cambridge: Cambridge University Press, 2004, 159–69.

44. Plato, *Euthyphro*. In *Readings in Ancient Greek Philosophy*, 2nd edition, edited by S. Marc Cohen and Patricia Curd, translated by C. D. C. Reeve, 97–114. Indianapolis: Hackett Publishing, 2005.

45. Quinn, Philip. *Divine Commands and Moral Requirements*. Oxford: Clarendon Library of Logic and Philosophy, 1978.

46. Rawls, John. *A Theory of Justice*. Cambridge, MA: Harvard University Press, 1971.

47. Richter, D. J. *Ethics after Anscombe: Post "Modern Moral Philosophy"*. Dordrecht: Springer Publishers, 2000.

48. Russell, Daniel C., ed. *The Cambridge Companion to Virtue Ethics*. Cambridge: Cambridge University Press, 2013.

49. Schultz, Barton. "Henry Sidgwick." In *The Stanford Encyclopedia of Philosophy* (Summer 2015 edition), edited by Edward N. Zalta. Accessed October 7, 2015. http://stanford.library.usyd.edu.au/archives/sum2010/entries/sidgwick/.

50. Sidgwick, Henry. *Methods of Ethics*, 7th edition. Indianapolis: Hackett, 1981.

51. Singer, Peter. *Practical Ethics*. Cambridge: Cambridge University Press, 1979.

52. Sinnott-Armstrong, Walter, ed. *Moral Psychology. Vol. 1. The Evolution of Morality: Adaptations and Innateness*. Cambridge, MA: MIT, 2007.

53. Teichmann, Roger. *The Philosophy of Elizabeth Anscombe*. Oxford: Oxford University Press, 2008.

54. Williams, Bernard and J. J. C. Smart. *Utilitarianism: For and Against*. Cambridge: Cambridge University Press, 1973.

55. Wittgenstein, Ludwig. *Philosophical Investigations (Philosophische Untersuchungen) English & German*, trans. G. E. M. Anscombe. Oxford: Basil Blackwell, 1953).

56. ———. *Philosophical Investigations*, 4th edition, 2009. Edited and translated by P. M. S. Hacker and Joachim Schulte. Oxford: Wiley-Blackwell, 2009.

57. ———. *Tractatus Logico-Philosophicus*. Translated by D. F. Pears and B. F. McGuinness. London: Routledge & Kegan Paul, 1974.

原书作者简介

伊丽莎白·安斯康姆，又名 G. E. M. 安斯康姆，出生于 1919 年，20 世纪英国主要哲学家之一。先就学于牛津大学，后执教于牛津和剑桥大学。

安斯康姆师从奥地利哲学大师路德维希·维特根斯坦，在剑桥学习过他讲授的课程，并翻译了他的作品。安斯康姆是虔诚的罗马天主教徒，她不仅因哲学著作而声名卓著，她在一些伦理和政治问题上的道德立场也让她广为人知，例如她坚决反对避孕和核武器。她公开反对剑桥大学授予美国总统哈里·S. 杜鲁门荣誉学位，理由为杜鲁门在二战时期批准对日本的两个城市使用核武器。安斯康姆于 2001 年去世，享年 81 岁。

本书作者简介

乔尼·布莱米博士，于伦敦大学国王学院获哲学博士学位，研究领域为概率哲学和认识论哲学。

乔恩·汤普森，目前在伦敦大学国王学院哲学系从事科研工作。

世界名著中的批判性思维

《世界思想宝库钥匙丛书》致力于深入浅出地阐释全世界著名思想家的观点，不论是谁、在何处都能了解到，从而推进批判性思维发展。

《世界思想宝库钥匙丛书》与世界顶尖大学的一流学者合作，为一系列学科中最有影响的著作推出新的分析文本，介绍其观点和影响。在这一不断扩展的系列中，每种选入的著作都代表了历经时间考验的思想典范。通过为这些著作提供必要背景、揭示原作者的学术渊源以及说明这些著作所产生的影响，本系列图书希望让读者以新视角看待这些划时代的经典之作。读者应学会思考、运用并挑战这些著作中的观点，而不是简单接受它们。

ABOUT THE AUTHOR OF THE ORIGINAL WORK

Elizabeth Anscombe—also known as G. E. M. Anscombe—was born in 1919, and was a major British philosopher of the twentieth century. She studied at Oxford and subsequently taught both there and at the University of Cambridge.

Anscombe was a follower of the celebrated Austrian philosopher Ludwig Wittgenstein and attended his lectures at Cambridge, later translating his work. A devout Roman Catholic, she was renowned not only for her philosophical work but also for her moral stance on several ethical and political issues, including opposition to contraception and nuclear weapons. She publicly opposed the honorary degree awarded by Oxford to US President Harry S. Truman on the grounds that he had approved the dropping of nuclear bombs on Japanese cities in World War II. Anscombe died in 2001 at the age of 81.

ABOUT THE AUTHORS OF THE ANALYSIS

Dr Jonny Blamey received his PhD in philosophy from King's College London. His work focuses on the philosophy of probability and epistemology.

Jon Thompson currently researches in the philosophy department at King's College London.

ABOUT MACAT
GREAT WORKS FOR CRITICAL THINKING

Macat is focused on making the ideas of the world's great thinkers accessible and comprehensible to everybody, everywhere, in ways that promote the development of enhanced critical thinking skills.

It works with leading academics from the world's top universities to produce new analyses that focus on the ideas and the impact of the most influential works ever written across a wide variety of academic disciplines. Each of the works that sit at the heart of its growing library is an enduring example of great thinking. But by setting them in context — and looking at the influences that shaped their authors, as well as the responses they provoked — Macat encourages readers to look at these classics and game-changers with fresh eyes. Readers learn to think, engage and challenge their ideas, rather than simply accepting them.

批判性思维与《现代道德哲学》

首要批判性思维技巧：评价

次要批判性思维技巧：分析

伊丽莎白·安斯康姆 1958 年的文章《现代道德哲学》是现代哲学史上划时代的作品，充分体现出优秀的批判性思维所具备的评价和分析能力。

虽然仅有 16 页，安斯康姆的文章却改变了整个现代道德哲学领域——要做到这一点，只能通过细致考察该领域巨擘们的已有观点。为此，她使用了评价和分析的核心技巧。

在批判性思维中，分析有助于理解观点的次序与特征：它考察这些观点基于何种理由，具有何种隐藏的理由和假设，最终得出何种结论。评价指判断观点是否足以支撑其结论：它考察所提供的理由是否可信、充分和相关，以及基于这些理由的结论是否有效。

在《现代道德哲学》中，安斯康姆冷静地运用这些技巧分析 18 世纪以来统治道德哲学的人物，揭露其作品潜在的假设、其缺点和优点，并证明这些道德哲学之间所谓的观点差异在很多方面而言其实微乎其微。《现代道德哲学》是一篇极具深度的优秀论文，极大地影响了其所属的领域，尽管不乏争议，但至今仍需阅读。

CRITICAL THINKING AND "MODERN MORAL PHILOSOPHY"

- Primary critical thinking skill: EVALUATION
- Secondary critical thinking skill: ANALYSIS

Elizabeth Anscombe's 1958 essay "Modern Moral Philosophy" is a cutting intervention in modern philosophy that shows the full power of good evaluative and analytical critical thinking skills.

Though only 16 pages long, Anscombe's paper set out to do nothing less than reform the entire field of modern moral philosophy—something that could only be done by carefully examining the existing arguments of the giants of the field. To do this, she deployed the central skills of evaluation and analysis.

In critical thinking, analysis helps understand the sequence and features of arguments: it asks what reasons these arguments produce, what implicit reasons and assumptions they rely on, what conclusions they arrive at. Evaluation involves judging whether or not the arguments are strong enough to sustain their conclusions: it asks how acceptable, adequate, and relevant the reasons given are, and whether or not the conclusions drawn from them are really valid.

In "Modern Moral Philosophy,"Anscombe dispassionately turns these skills on figures that have dominated moral philosophy since the 18th-century, revealing the underlying assumptions of their work, their weaknesses and strengths, and showing that in many ways the supposed differences between their arguments are actually negligible. A brilliantly incisive piece,"Modern Moral Philosophy" radically affected its field, remaining required—and controversial—reading today.

《世界思想宝库钥匙丛书》简介

　　《世界思想宝库钥匙丛书》致力于为一系列在各领域产生重大影响的人文社科类经典著作提供独特的学术探讨。每一本读物都不仅仅是原经典著作的内容摘要，而是介绍并深入研究原经典著作的学术渊源、主要观点和历史影响。这一丛书的目的是提供一套学习资料，以促进读者掌握批判性思维，从而更全面、深刻地去理解重要思想。

　　每一本读物分为 3 个部分：学术渊源、学术思想和学术影响，每个部分下有 4 个小节。这些章节旨在从各个方面研究原经典著作及其反响。

　　由于独特的体例，每一本读物不但易于阅读，而且另有一项优点：所有读物的编排体例相同，读者在进行某个知识层面的调查或研究时可交叉参阅多本该丛书中的相关读物，从而开启跨领域研究的路径。

　　为了方便阅读，每本读物最后还列出了术语表和人名表（在书中则以星号＊标记），此外还有参考文献。

　　《世界思想宝库钥匙丛书》与剑桥大学合作，理清了批判性思维的要点，即如何通过 6 种技能来进行有效思考。其中 3 种技能让我们能够理解问题，另 3 种技能让我们有能力解决问题。这 6 种技能合称为"批判性思维 PACIER 模式"，它们是：

分析：了解如何建立一个观点；
评估：研究一个观点的优点和缺点；
阐释：对意义所产生的问题加以理解；
创造性思维：提出新的见解，发现新的联系；
解决问题：提出切实有效的解决办法；
理性化思维：创建有说服力的观点。

THE MACAT LIBRARY

The Macat Library is a series of unique academic explorations of seminal works in the humanities and social sciences — books and papers that have had a significant and widely recognised impact on their disciplines. It has been created to serve as much more than just a summary of what lies between the covers of a great book. It illuminates and explores the influences on, ideas of, and impact of that book. Our goal is to offer a learning resource that encourages critical thinking and fosters a better, deeper understanding of important ideas.

Each publication is divided into three Sections: Influences, Ideas, and Impact. Each Section has four Modules. These explore every important facet of the work, and the responses to it.

This Section-Module structure makes a Macat Library book easy to use, but it has another important feature. Because each Macat book is written to the same format, it is possible (and encouraged!) to cross-reference multiple Macat books along the same lines of inquiry or research. This allows the reader to open up interesting interdisciplinary pathways.

To further aid your reading, lists of glossary terms and people mentioned are included at the end of this book (these are indicated by an asterisk [*] throughout) — as well as a list of works cited.

Macat has worked with the University of Cambridge to identify the elements of critical thinking and understand the ways in which six different skills combine to enable effective thinking.

Three allow us to fully understand a problem; three more give us the tools to solve it. Together, these six skills make up the PACIER model of critical thinking. They are:

ANALYSIS — understanding how an argument is built
EVALUATION — exploring the strengths and weaknesses of an argument
INTERPRETATION — understanding issues of meaning
CREATIVE THINKING — coming up with new ideas and fresh connections
PROBLEM-SOLVING — producing strong solutions
REASONING — creating strong arguments

"《世界思想宝库钥匙丛书》提供了独一无二的跨学科学习和研究工具。它介绍那些革新了各自学科研究的经典著作，还邀请全世界一流专家和教育机构进行严谨的分析，为每位读者打开世界顶级教育的大门。"

—— 安德烈亚斯·施莱歇尔，
经济合作与发展组织教育与技能司司长

"《世界思想宝库钥匙丛书》直面大学教育的巨大挑战……他们组建了一支精干而活跃的学者队伍，来推出在研究广度上颇具新意的教学材料。"

—— 布罗尔斯教授、勋爵，剑桥大学前校长

"《世界思想宝库钥匙丛书》的愿景令人赞叹。它通过分析和阐释那些曾深刻影响人类思想以及社会、经济发展的经典文本，提供了新的学习方法。它推动批判性思维，这对于任何社会和经济体来说都是至关重要的。这就是未来的学习方法。"

—— 查尔斯·克拉克阁下，英国前教育大臣

"对于那些影响了各自领域的著作，《世界思想宝库钥匙丛书》能让人们立即了解到围绕那些著作展开的评论性言论，这让该系列图书成为在这些领域从事研究的师生们不可或缺的资源。"

—— 威廉·特朗佐教授，加利福尼亚大学圣地亚哥分校

"Macat offers an amazing first-of-its-kind tool for interdisciplinary learning and research. Its focus on works that transformed their disciplines and its rigorous approach, drawing on the world's leading experts and educational institutions, opens up a world-class education to anyone."

—— Andreas Schleicher, Director for Education and Skills, Organisation for Economic Co-operation and Development

"Macat is taking on some of the major challenges in university education... They have drawn together a strong team of active academics who are producing teaching materials that are novel in the breadth of their approach."

—— Prof Lord Broers, former Vice-Chancellor of the University of Cambridge

"The Macat vision is exceptionally exciting. It focuses upon new modes of learning which analyse and explain seminal texts which have profoundly influenced world thinking and so social and economic development. It promotes the kind of critical thinking which is essential for any society and economy. This is the learning of the future."

—— Rt Hon Charles Clarke, former UK Secretary of State for Education

"The Macat analyses provide immediate access to the critical conversation surrounding the books that have shaped their respective discipline, which will make them an invaluable resource to all of those, students and teachers, working in the field."

—— Prof William Tronzo, University of California at San Diego

♀ The Macat Library
世界思想宝库钥匙丛书

TITLE	中文书名	类别
An Analysis of Arjun Appadurai's *Modernity at Large: Cultural Dimensions of Globalization*	解析阿尔君·阿帕杜莱《消失的现代性：全球化的文化维度》	人类学
An Analysis of Claude Lévi-Strauss's *Structural Anthropology*	解析克劳德·列维-斯特劳斯《结构人类学》	人类学
An Analysis of Marcel Mauss's *The Gift*	解析马塞尔·莫斯《礼物》	人类学
An Analysis of Jared M. Diamond's *Guns, Germs, and Steel: The Fate of Human Societies*	解析贾雷德·M.戴蒙德《枪炮、病菌与钢铁：人类社会的命运》	人类学
An Analysis of Clifford Geertz's *The Interpretation of Cultures*	解析克利福德·格尔茨《文化的解释》	人类学
An Analysis of Philippe Ariès's *Centuries of Childhood: A Social History of Family Life*	解析菲力浦·阿利埃斯《儿童的世纪：旧制度下的儿童和家庭生活》	人类学
An Analysis of W. Chan Kim & Renée Mauborgne's *Blue Ocean Strategy*	解析金伟灿/勒妮·莫博涅《蓝海战略》	商业
An Analysis of John P. Kotter's *Leading Change*	解析约翰·P.科特《领导变革》	商业
An Analysis of Michael E. Porter's *Competitive Strategy: Techniques for Analyzing Industries and Competitors*	解析迈克尔·E.波特《竞争战略：分析产业和竞争对手的技术》	商业
An Analysis of Jean Lave & Etienne Wenger's *Situated Learning: Legitimate Peripheral Participation*	解析琼·莱夫/艾蒂纳·温格《情境学习：合法的边缘性参与》	商业
An Analysis of Douglas McGregor's *The Human Side of Enterprise*	解析道格拉斯·麦格雷戈《企业的人性面》	商业
An Analysis of Milton Friedman's *Capitalism and Freedom*	解析米尔顿·弗里德曼《资本主义与自由》	商业
An Analysis of Ludwig von Mises's *The Theory of Money and Credit*	解析路德维希·冯·米塞斯《货币和信用理论》	经济学
An Analysis of Adam Smith's *The Wealth of Nations*	解析亚当·斯密《国富论》	经济学
An Analysis of Thomas Piketty's *Capital in the Twenty-First Century*	解析托马斯·皮凯蒂《21世纪资本论》	经济学
An Analysis of Nassim Nicholas Taleb's *The Black Swan: The Impact of the Highly Improbable*	解析纳西姆·尼古拉斯·塔勒布《黑天鹅：如何应对不可预知的未来》	经济学
An Analysis of Ha-Joon Chang's *Kicking Away the Ladder*	解析张夏准《富国陷阱：发达国家为何踢开梯子》	经济学
An Analysis of Thomas Robert Malthus's *An Essay on the Principle of Population*	解析托马斯·罗伯特·马尔萨斯《人口论》	经济学

An Analysis of John Maynard Keynes's *The General Theory of Employment, Interest and Money*	解析约翰·梅纳德·凯恩斯《就业、利息和货币通论》	经济学
An Analysis of Milton Friedman's *The Role of Monetary Policy*	解析米尔顿·弗里德曼《货币政策的作用》	经济学
An Analysis of Burton G. Malkiel's *A Random Walk Down Wall Street*	解析伯顿·G.马尔基尔《漫步华尔街》	经济学
An Analysis of Friedrich A. Hayek's *The Road to Serfdom*	解析弗里德里希·A.哈耶克《通往奴役之路》	经济学
An Analysis of Charles P. Kindleberger's *Manias, Panics, and Crashes: A History of Financial Crises*	解析查尔斯·P.金德尔伯格《疯狂、惊恐和崩溃：金融危机史》	经济学
An Analysis of Amartya Sen's *Development as Freedom*	解析阿马蒂亚·森《以自由看待发展》	经济学
An Analysis of Rachel Carson's *Silent Spring*	解析蕾切尔·卡森《寂静的春天》	地理学
An Analysis of Charles Darwin's *On the Origin of Species: by Means of Natural Selection, or The Preservation of Favoured Races in the Struggle for Life*	解析查尔斯·达尔文《物种起源》	地理学
An Analysis of World Commission on Environment and Development's *The Brundtland Report, Our Common Future*	解析世界环境与发展委员会《布伦特兰报告：我们共同的未来》	地理学
An Analysis of James E. Lovelock's *Gaia: A New Look at Life on Earth*	解析詹姆斯·E.拉伍洛克《盖娅：地球生命的新视野》	地理学
An Analysis of Paul Kennedy's *The Rise and Fall of the Great Powers: Economic Change and Military Conflict from 1500–2000*	解析保罗·肯尼迪《大国的兴衰：1500—2000年的经济变革与军事冲突》	历史
An Analysis of Janet L. Abu-Lughod's *Before European Hegemony: The World System A. D. 1250–1350*	解析珍妮特·L.阿布-卢格霍德《欧洲霸权之前：1250—1350年的世界体系》	历史
An Analysis of Alfred W. Crosby's *The Columbian Exchange: Biological and Cultural Consequences of 1492*	解析艾尔弗雷德·W.克罗斯比《哥伦布大交换：1492年以后的生物影响和文化冲击》	历史
An Analysis of Tony Judt's *Postwar: A History of Europe since 1945*	解析托尼·朱特《战后欧洲史》	历史
An Analysis of Richard J. Evans's *In Defence of History*	解析理查德·J.艾文斯《捍卫历史》	历史
An Analysis of Eric Hobsbawm's *The Age of Revolution: Europe 1789–1848*	解析艾瑞克·霍布斯鲍姆《革命的年代：欧洲1789—1848年》	历史

An Analysis of Roland Barthes's *Mythologies*	解析罗兰·巴特《神话学》	文学与批判理论
An Analysis of Simone de Beauvoir's *The Second Sex*	解析西蒙娜·德·波伏娃《第二性》	文学与批判理论
An Analysis of Edward W. Said's *Orientalism*	解析爱德华·W. 萨义德《东方主义》	文学与批判理论
An Analysis of Virginia Woolf's *A Room of One's Own*	解析弗吉尼亚·伍尔芙《一间自己的房间》	文学与批判理论
An Analysis of Judith Butler's *Gender Trouble*	解析朱迪斯·巴特勒《性别麻烦》	文学与批判理论
An Analysis of Ferdinand de Saussure's *Course in General Linguistics*	解析费尔迪南·德·索绪尔《普通语言学教程》	文学与批判理论
An Analysis of Susan Sontag's *On Photography*	解析苏珊·桑塔格《论摄影》	文学与批判理论
An Analysis of Walter Benjamin's *The Work of Art in the Age of Mechanical Reproduction*	解析瓦尔特·本雅明《机械复制时代的艺术作品》	文学与批判理论
An Analysis of W. E. B. Du Bois's *The Souls of Black Folk*	解析 W.E.B. 杜波依斯《黑人的灵魂》	文学与批判理论
An Analysis of Plato's *The Republic*	解析柏拉图《理想国》	哲学
An Analysis of Plato's *Symposium*	解析柏拉图《会饮篇》	哲学
An Analysis of Aristotle's *Metaphysics*	解析亚里士多德《形而上学》	哲学
An Analysis of Aristotle's *Nicomachean Ethics*	解析亚里士多德《尼各马可伦理学》	哲学
An Analysis of Immanuel Kant's *Critique of Pure Reason*	解析伊曼努尔·康德《纯粹理性批判》	哲学
An Analysis of Ludwig Wittgenstein's *Philosophical Investigations*	解析路德维希·维特根斯坦《哲学研究》	哲学
An Analysis of G. W. F. Hegel's *Phenomenology of Spirit*	解析 G. W. F. 黑格尔《精神现象学》	哲学
An Analysis of Baruch Spinoza's *Ethics*	解析巴鲁赫·斯宾诺莎《伦理学》	哲学
An Analysis of Hannah Arendt's *The Human Condition*	解析汉娜·阿伦特《人的境况》	哲学
An Analysis of G. E. M. Anscombe's *Modern Moral Philosophy*	解析 G. E. M. 安斯康姆《现代道德哲学》	哲学
An Analysis of David Hume's *An Enquiry Concerning Human Understanding*	解析大卫·休谟《人类理解研究》	哲学

An Analysis of Søren Kierkegaard's *Fear and Trembling*	解析索伦·克尔凯郭尔《恐惧与战栗》	哲学
An Analysis of René Descartes's *Meditations on First Philosophy*	解析勒内·笛卡尔《第一哲学沉思录》	哲学
An Analysis of Friedrich Nietzsche's *On the Genealogy of Morality*	解析弗里德里希·尼采《论道德的谱系》	哲学
An Analysis of Gilbert Ryle's *The Concept of Mind*	解析吉尔伯特·赖尔《心的概念》	哲学
An Analysis of Thomas Kuhn's *The Structure of Scientific Revolutions*	解析托马斯·库恩《科学革命的结构》	哲学
An Analysis of John Stuart Mill's *Utilitarianism*	解析约翰·斯图亚特·穆勒《功利主义》	哲学
An Analysis of Aristotle's *Politics*	解析亚里士多德《政治学》	政治学
An Analysis of Niccolò Machiavelli's *The Prince*	解析尼科洛·马基雅维利《君主论》	政治学
An Analysis of Karl Marx's *Capital*	解析卡尔·马克思《资本论》	政治学
An Analysis of Benedict Anderson's *Imagined Communities*	解析本尼迪克特·安德森《想象的共同体》	政治学
An Analysis of Samuel P. Huntington's *The Clash of Civilizations and the Remaking of World Order*	解析塞缪尔·P.亨廷顿《文明的冲突与世界秩序的重建》	政治学
An Analysis of Alexis de Tocqueville's *Democracy in America*	解析阿列克西·德·托克维尔《论美国的民主》	政治学
An Analysis of John A. Hobson's *Imperialism: A Study*	解析约翰·A.霍布森《帝国主义》	政治学
An Analysis of Thomas Paine's *Common Sense*	解析托马斯·潘恩《常识》	政治学
An Analysis of John Rawls's *A Theory of Justice*	解析约翰·罗尔斯《正义论》	政治学
An Analysis of Francis Fukuyama's *The End of History and the Last Man*	解析弗朗西斯·福山《历史的终结与最后的人》	政治学
An Analysis of John Locke's *Two Treatises of Government*	解析约翰·洛克《政府论》	政治学
An Analysis of Sun Tzu's *The Art of War*	解析孙武《孙子兵法》	政治学
An Analysis of Henry Kissinger's *World Order: Reflections on the Character of Nations and the Course of History*	解析亨利·基辛格《世界秩序》	政治学
An Analysis of Jean-Jacques Rousseau's *The Social Contract*	解析让-雅克·卢梭《社会契约论》	政治学

An Analysis of Odd Arne Westad's *The Global Cold War: Third World Interventions and the Making of Our Times*	解析文安立《全球冷战：美苏对第三世界的干涉与当代世界的形成》	政治学
An Analysis of Sigmund Freud's *The Interpretation of Dreams*	解析西格蒙德·弗洛伊德《梦的解析》	心理学
An Analysis of William James' *The Principles of Psychology*	解析威廉·詹姆斯《心理学原理》	心理学
An Analysis of Philip Zimbardo's *The Lucifer Effect*	解析菲利普·津巴多《路西法效应》	心理学
An Analysis of Leon Festinger's *A Theory of Cognitive Dissonance*	解析利昂·费斯汀格《认知失调论》	心理学
An Analysis of Richard H. Thaler & Cass R. Sunstein's *Nudge: Improving Decisions about Health, Wealth, and Happiness*	解析理查德·H.泰勒/卡斯·R.桑斯坦《助推：如何做出有关健康、财富和幸福的更优决策》	心理学
An Analysis of Gordon Allport's *The Nature of Prejudice*	解析高尔登·奥尔波特《偏见的本质》	心理学
An Analysis of Steven Pinker's *The Better Angels of Our Nature: Why Violence Has Declined*	解析斯蒂芬·平克《人性中的善良天使：暴力为什么会减少》	心理学
An Analysis of Stanley Milgram's *Obedience to Authority*	解析斯坦利·米尔格拉姆《对权威的服从》	心理学
An Analysis of Betty Friedan's *The Feminine Mystique*	解析贝蒂·弗里丹《女性的奥秘》	心理学
An Analysis of David Riesman's *The Lonely Crowd: A Study of the Changing American Character*	解析大卫·理斯曼《孤独的人群：美国人社会性格演变之研究》	社会学
An Analysis of Franz Boas's *Race, Language and Culture*	解析弗朗兹·博厄斯《种族、语言与文化》	社会学
An Analysis of Pierre Bourdieu's *Outline of a Theory of Practice*	解析皮埃尔·布尔迪厄《实践理论大纲》	社会学
An Analysis of Max Weber's *The Protestant Ethic and the Spirit of Capitalism*	解析马克斯·韦伯《新教伦理与资本主义精神》	社会学
An Analysis of Jane Jacobs's *The Death and Life of Great American Cities*	解析简·雅各布斯《美国大城市的死与生》	社会学
An Analysis of C. Wright Mills's *The Sociological Imagination*	解析C.赖特·米尔斯《社会学的想象力》	社会学
An Analysis of Robert E. Lucas Jr.'s *Why Doesn't Capital Flow from Rich to Poor Countries?*	解析小罗伯特·E.卢卡斯《为何资本不从富国流向穷国？》	社会学

An Analysis of Émile Durkheim's *On Suicide*	解析埃米尔·迪尔凯姆《自杀论》	社会学
An Analysis of Eric Hoffer's *The True Believer: Thoughts on the Nature of Mass Movements*	解析埃里克·霍弗《狂热分子：群众运动圣经》	社会学
An Analysis of Jared M. Diamond's *Collapse: How Societies Choose to Fail or Survive*	解析贾雷德·M.戴蒙德《大崩溃：社会如何选择兴亡》	社会学
An Analysis of Michel Foucault's *The History of Sexuality Vol. 1: The Will to Knowledge*	解析米歇尔·福柯《性史（第一卷）：求知意志》	社会学
An Analysis of Michel Foucault's *Discipline and Punish*	解析米歇尔·福柯《规训与惩罚》	社会学
An Analysis of Richard Dawkins's *The Selfish Gene*	解析理查德·道金斯《自私的基因》	社会学
An Analysis of Antonio Gramsci's *Prison Notebooks*	解析安东尼奥·葛兰西《狱中札记》	社会学
An Analysis of Augustine's *Confessions*	解析奥古斯丁《忏悔录》	神学
An Analysis of C. S. Lewis's *The Abolition of Man*	解析 C. S. 路易斯《人之废》	神学

图书在版编目（CIP）数据

解析G. E. M. 安斯康姆《现代道德哲学》: 汉、英 / 乔尼·布莱米（Jonny Blame
乔恩·汤普森（Jon Thompson）著；陈广兴译 . —上海：上海外语教育出版社，2
（世界思想宝库钥匙丛书）
ISBN 978 - 7 - 5446 - 6120 - 1

Ⅰ.①解… Ⅱ.①乔… ②乔… ③陈… Ⅲ.①伊丽莎白·安斯康姆（Gertrude Elizal
Margaret Anscombe 1919—2001）-伦理学-研究 Ⅳ.①B561.59 ②B82

中国版本图书馆CIP数据核字（2020）第014509号

This Chinese-English bilingual edition of *An Analysis of G. E. M. Anscombe's* Modern Moral
Philosophy is published by arrangement with Macat International Limited.
Licensed for sale throughout the world.

本书汉英双语版由Macat国际有限公司授权上海外语教育出版社有限公司出版。
供在全世界范围内发行、销售。

图字：09 - 2018 - 549

出版发行：**上海外语教育出版社**
　　　　　　（上海外国语大学内）　邮编：200083
电　　话：021-65425300（总机）
电子邮箱：bookinfo@sflep.com.cn
网　　址：http://www.sflep.com
责任编辑：杨莹雪

印　　刷：上海信老印刷厂
开　　本：890×1240　1/32　印张 5.375　字数 111千字
版　　次：2020 年 6 月第 1 版　 2020 年 6 月第 1 次印刷
印　　数：2 100 册

书　　号：ISBN 978-7-5446-6120-1
定　　价：30.00 元

本版图书如有印装质量问题，可向本社调换
质量服务热线：4008-213-263　电子邮箱：editorial@sflep.com